Making Magic with
GAIA

Making Magic with

GAIA

PRACTICES TO HEAL OURSELVES
AND OUR PLANET

Francesca Ciancimino Howell

Ostara 2004

Blessings & joy !

Francesca Ciancimino Howell

Red Wheel
Boston, MA / York Beach, ME

First published in 2002 by
Red Wheel/Weiser, LLC
York Beach, ME
With offices at:
368 Congress Street
Boston, MA 02210
www.redwheelweiser.com

Library of Congress Cataloging-in-Publication Data

Howell, Francesca.
    Making magic with Gaia : practices to heal ourselves and our planet /
Francesca Howell.
        p. cm.
    Includes bibliographical references.
    ISBN 1-59003-008-7 (pbk. : alk. paper)
    1. Magic. 2. Nature—Miscellanea. I. Title.

BF1621 .H69 2002   2001048724

133.4'3—dc21

Typeset in 10/12 Minion

Printed in the Canada

TCP

09 08 07 06 05 04 03 02
8   7   6   5   4   3   2   1

The paper used in this publication meets the minimum requirements of the American National Standard for Information Sciences—Permanence of Paper for Printed Library Materials Z39.48-1992 (R1997).

To my exceptional husband, my magnificent children, and my beautiful mother.

And, of course, with love to Gaia.

Great Goddess—
May we through our
devotion, love, and work
reveal to all the temple
that is our Mother Earth

Francesca C. Howell, 1995

Contents

Acknowledgments

First I must thank my family. My exceptional husband, Peter, has been a constant font of support, inspiration, and encouragement in our twenty-two years together. He has aided me invaluably in developing my various creative interests, not the least of which is my writing. My two beautiful, loving children also have been true sources of inspiration and motivation as they illustrate the compelling reason we must care for our Mother Planet—the generations to come.

My sister and my mother have not only been supportive, but also serve as shining examples of ecumenism and religious tolerance. My sister is a member of an order of Franciscan nuns, and my mother is a devout Catholic. Yet they understand and accept my beliefs, and we recognize jointly that there are many paths to Divine Truth.

I am grateful for the blessing that brought me my publisher, Jan Johnson, and all at Red Wheel/Weiser. Jan heard Gaia's voice and helped to midwife this book's appearance in the world with superb intuition and sensitivity. I also must thank Caroline Pincus for her editing and midwifery on the later drafts.

Next I want to express my gratitude to Myrddin and Crystal, founding Elders of the Gaia Group for their teachings and support over many years. (And always for their wonderful senses of humor!)

Vivianne and Chris Crowley have also been superb role models and inspirations. Although I am not their Initiate, they generously invited me to work magically with their coven, the Aurora Aurea, in the U.K., for more than five years. Thus my Temple of Gaia is not only the daughter of the Gaia Group but is also a "Goddess Child" of the Aurora Aurea.

The members of the Temple of Gaia, past and present, have contributed in no small part to this book with their creativity in spells, rituals, and superb magical activism. Thank you all.

I am grateful for having found Unitarian Universalism. Its time-honored traditions of activism and dedication to human rights, civil rights, and environmentalism have aided me in continuing to "walk my talk." The Rev. Kurt Kuhwald, the Unitarian Universalist Church of Boulder, Colorado, and the Rev. Jacqueline Ziegler have also helped me to grow in this work. Kurt, Jackie, and various members of the Boulder Church have validated my Wiccan "ministry" in the larger community, giving me a sense of having a voice worth hearing by all, not only Wiccans.

My thanks go out to many other friends for their help, support, and artistic advice. In particular I should mention Chris Hoffman, author and ecopsychologist, who provided excellent editing. My gratitude goes out to all those who have sustained my journey, even if it was only through a smile or a kind word. No act of kindness and compassion is small.

My gratitude and eternal admiration go to the legions of activists and environmental crusaders who work day in and day out for Gaia and for us all, some nameless and some well known. Like the now-renowned Julia Butterfly Hill, who lived for two years in the branches of the giant redwood tree "Luna" in order to protect the forests of the northwestern United States, these activists take risks and make sacrifices many of us would never dare.

I would like to thank Anya Beebe for permission to use her dedication poem on page 123.

For permission to use copyright material, I gratefully make the following acknowledgments:

HarperCollins Publishers, Ltd. for permission to use "The Pipes of Pan" from *Wicca: The Old Religion in the New Millennium* by Vivianne Crowley, published by Thorssons, 1996.

The Society of Authors as the Literary Representative of the Estate of Rose Fyleman for permission to use "The Fairies Have Never a Penny to Spend" by Rose Fyleman first published in *Fairies and Chimneys* by Doubleday and Company, Inc., 1920.

Introduction

The concept of wilderness needs no defense,
simply more defenders.

Edward Abbey

You are about to enter into a mysterious, joyful, and fantastically rewarding community of those in touch with Mother Earth in the deepest and
most healing way. Your community will grow to encompass not only fellow humans, but many other species and nonhuman beings as well.
(That is, of course, if it does not already include them!) The Ancient
Gods, the Shining Ones, the Faery Folk, or perhaps Dragons, Totem
Animals—whoever or whatever you wish to encounter in the service of
Mother Earth can become your companions. I bless and honor all of you,
coming from whatever tradition you may hail . . . whatever nationality,
race, political philosophy, sexual preference. Welcome. Gaia, our Mother
Planet, desperately needs our aid.

In recent years, some members of the U.S. Congress have tried to
create sentiment against environmental legislation by calling environmentalists "Pagans," as if the word were an epithet. The truth is, many
environmentalists are Pagans. Not all, certainly, but many. Why? Because
the Pagan worldview is based on the idea that all life is deeply interconnected and that stewardship of the earth is a form of spiritual practice.
In fact, in my spiritual tradition, which springs from the ancient Earth
religion currently known as Wicca, we actually take vows to make serv-
ing the earth part of our ministry.

Of course many paths and traditions—from Christianity to Judaism
to Buddhism—recognize and honor the interconnectedness of all life. I
have worked to heal the earth with many wonderful people, across
America and across the world, of differing perspectives and faiths. My
purpose in writing this book is not to convert anyone to Paganism or
Wicca, but to show how certain spiritual practices drawn from the
ancient magical arts can help to heal our mother Gaia. Among these are
techniques for meditation, trance work, creating sacred space, methods
of channeling energy to spread blessings to the environment, and finally
using magic to directly influence global issues. I will also offer ideas for
practices large and small that both attune you to the earth and directly

serve her in practical ways—recycling, composting, using sustainable practices of all kinds. Other suggestions and techniques aim to help those who love Gaia to become spiritual activists, true Rainbow Warriors whose goals are transformation and healing. At the root of all these actions is a magnificent feedback loop: in healing the earth, we can heal ourselves. In some ways, you might think of this book as a magical activist's handbook.

John Muir, one of the founders of the environmental movement in North America and of America's National Park system in the late nineteenth and early twentieth centuries, said: "Climb the mountains and get their good tidings. Nature's peace will flow into you as the sunshine flows into trees. The winds will blow their own freshness into you, and the storms their energy, while cares will drop off like autumn leaves."

Muir was essentially a Deep Ecologist by today's standards, though certainly he would not be called a Shaman or an Earth Magician. However, he was a great naturalist, and therefore, like generations of people who have loved and understood Nature, he recognized the gifts that Mother Gaia offers us when we seek out active contact with her.

I must warn you that some people will see this book as subversive. At worst it might be seen as dangerous and at least as "seriously out there." And you have just picked it up. Congratulations. Thank you for your act of faith. Perhaps you too have felt the calling from Nature, from your own experiences of peace and joy and enchantment while enjoying the earth's many gifts.

You may wonder who I am and how I came to write this book. I am a professional, a suburban "soccer mom," and a Third Degree High Priestess of the earth-centered tradition known as Wicca. (Believe me, it is not always easy to straddle these roles and worlds.) Along the way I've had a few exciting jobs, plus a career as an actress. I have performed on stage and on screen across the world; I have also hung off monumental cooling towers, chained myself to toxic waste sites, and marched in huge antiwar protests.

Personally I think saving dolphins is a lot more interesting—and fulfilling—than acting. For example, after years of acting training, followed by international TV and theater experience, I found myself once again confronted with simplistic scripts where my cleavage was more important than my character's intelligence. At the same time, the oil tanker *Exxon Valdez* sank in Prince William Sound, contaminating pristine wilderness with more than 11 million gallons of oil. The choice of professions became clear to me: the commercial acting world created by modern Western society no longer offered me a chance for service to the world, for inspiration or transformation. And our beautiful planet was in dire need. I applied to Greenpeace and the die was cast. Soap operas were never this exciting.

Now, if you're new to Wicca and the word *witch* still conjures up images of odd women in black pointy hats who do strange things with brooms, let me say this: yes, we sometimes do wear the hats and frequently use the brooms (often for deeply occult activities such as sweeping . . . among other things). However, today Witches are just as likely to be found in the classroom, boardroom, operating room, or, more to the point, sitting in trees in protest of logging operations or holding signs in front of the governor's office. A common slogan of American Witchcraft, "We are everywhere," is becoming truer by the day.

I believe in the effectiveness and importance of nonviolent direct actions of all kinds, in constant small acts of practical "green work" as well as in the work of spiritual healing. The practical and the magical are bound up, as the sacred permeates the mundane in life. Activism and magic, on any level, lead to bigger and bigger effects.

I undertook my first activist intervention, or "Direct Action," when I was eleven. I had not yet read Edward Abbey's *The Monkey Wrench Gang*, nor did I know what a Direct Action was. All I knew was that the beautiful woodlands and meadows where my friends and I kept our horses were about to be bulldozed, and I wanted to stop that. It was the Vietnam era and we had heard of sit-ins, so my friends and I sat around the bulldozers and wouldn't move.

As you can imagine, we didn't stop the destruction of those woods, with their bear and deer and clear bubbling springs I loved so. However, while some of our classmates had started to hang out in those new suburban abominations known as shopping malls, my preteen friends and I had begun to develop an activist attitude of standing up for the environment.

We also knew of "Witchcraft's" practices of herbalism and tarot, the use of meditation and trance states, and belief in reincarnation. We had had the good fortune to meet an older teen who called herself a Witch and who taught us some of the techniques commonly known as "white magic." We practiced those ancient techniques when we were not riding our horses or going to junior high school. Contrary to Hollywood's characterization of teenage Witches, we did not try to put spells on anyone, but talking to trees and Elemental beings in the woods did lead us, young as we were, to environmental activism.

Others in my family were devout Catholics and were none too pleased when they discovered what I was up to, but I just couldn't see any conflict between the Catholicism I had been brought up with and my new nature-loving spiritual practices. My Irish American mother had raised me on her father's Celtic tales of Faery Folk (the "wee folk"), of talking animals and trees, and of the sacredness of all life. My father was Sicilian and my parents had named me after the Catholic patron saint of Nature, known in America as Francis of Assisi, whose real name was Francesco Bernardone. (I was born on his feast day.) Francesco, or Saint Francis, was a great mystic, the author of one of the earliest odes to Nature, and truly a forefather of Deep Ecology and Creation Spirituality.[1] As many readers will remember from Italian legend, he is said to have had the ability to communicate with animals and with the forces of Nature. In fact, he called them his brothers and sisters. As far as I was concerned, it would have been a crime to ignore, or worse, to devastate Nature's loveliness as humanity has been wont to do.

I have learned quite a few things since those early days, of course, but one thing remains clear: Mother Earth needs our help. As people of spirit and conscience, we must see our stewardship toward her as an essential part of our spiritual practice, which leads to a huge circle of energy, as portrayed by the ancient symbol of the snake biting its tail, the Ouroboros. As our magical practice and relationships with the Gods and Elementals (Nature spirits, Faery Folk, those beings close to the earth and to humanity but not visible to humans) attune us to Gaia's needs, they also fuel us with the requisite "fire in the belly" to do our work in the world.

The magical practices I offer here can serve to protect the practitioner from two dangers that activists face: (1) burnout caused by spiritual or physical exhaustion, and (2) that old "I'm saving the earth, get out of my way" ego delusion. How does magic do this? Ritual and magic, our communication with the Gods and Goddesses, give us an inexhaustible supply of energy and provide spiritual grounding that helps keep us sane and centered. We can learn to access the true self, the authentic side of our internal nature through this kind of spiritual practice. And the intense and disciplined process of initiation into a mystery religion, such as Wicca, with its practices of contemplation, prayer, and meditation, can aid activists in avoiding the pitfalls of ego.

I do not propose to provide an extensive primer in magic, Wicca, or Witchcraft. Those readers interested in further study will find a list of recommended readings at the back of the book. It includes many wonderful offerings on rituals, spells, and magical practices. My intention here is to depict a unique "Earth Steward" spiritual path, the path of magical activism.

The practices outlined, when taken step by step, offer a safe and effective training program. Those who simply wish to connect more deeply with the earth without delving too much into magic and ritual may develop their own methods from those given and leave the rest. But make no mistake: this is an invitation and a call to action, a summoning from Gaia herself to aid in the healing of the earth and in the evolution of consciousness.

In the chapters that follow I offer meditations, visualizations or "pathworkings," rituals, and spells as examples of magical activism. I also include everyday practices that can reinforce and enhance our magical training. We will go from simple acts of meditation or practical work to more advanced magical work—all with the purpose of healing Gaia. The exercises and rituals come both from my own teaching practice and from my initiating tradition, the Gaia Group, and its Book of Shadows. (Book of Shadows, which I will often shorten to BoS, refers to the written collection of a Witch's or a coven's studies, rituals, spells, invocations, and so on. When a new member joins a tradition through initiation, he or she receives that tradition's BoS. Some of these teachings and spells derive from the communal origins of British and American Wicca.)

Gaia needs us. She is calling us, asking us to accept this ministry as our sacred duty. In the spirit of the Celtic Druids and the Priestesses at Delphi of long ago, I invite Initiates, dedicated Pagans, Deep Ecologists, environmental activists, Medicine Men and Women, Shamans, Earth Stewards, and all concerned individuals—whatever path or name they choose—to hear her voice, to step forward and make magic with Gaia.

Chapter 1
Hearing Gaia's Voice

I who am the beauty of the green Earth,
And the white moon among the stars,
And the mystery of the waters, . . .
I call upon thy soul to arise
And come unto me.
For I am the soul of Nature.

The Charge of the Goddess, *in the traditional Wiccan*
Book of Shadows

Nature is the greatest teacher and healer. People of all ages, beliefs, and cultures acknowledge the therapeutic qualities of sticking their hands in the earth, planting a garden, or taking a walk in Nature. Medical doctors have traditionally advised their patients to avail themselves of such benefits. Children know to do this instinctively, as the more intuitive, authentic beings they are. Witness how they love to collect rocks, pinecones, and other little gifts of the earth. Is there more to this than simply the healing effects of exercise and fresh air? Is there a force, an energy emanating from Mother Gaia, even through her smallest "representatives"—the rocks, wood, plants? I believe the answer is, without a doubt, yes.

In this chapter we'll look at how we can begin to communicate with Gaia, day in and day out, in our daily work on the spiritual and the practical planes. But first let's think about the word *Gaia* in its modern context.

In 1975 a renowned British scientist named Dr. James Lovelock, Fellow of the Royal Society, published a theory, based on his life's work and observations, proposing that Mother Earth is a living, self-regulating being. He called this intelligent life force "Gaia," in honor of the primordial Earth Mother of the Greeks. This "Gaia Hypothesis" became known worldwide and, to Lovelock's total surprise, was not attacked by the theological establishment as he had anticipated. It was, however, initially scoffed at by the scientific establishment.

Lovelock theorized that the presence of an intelligent, all-pervading life force shows itself in the many, well-balanced systems that regulate the health of our exquisitely unique planet. Not only does the atmosphere regulate itself constantly to maintain its heat-retaining properties, but the salinity of the seas also keeps itself within the appropriate range.

Together with his colleague Lynn Margulis, Lovelock demonstrated how Gaia's and our actions and life processes are interrelated and interdependent. He compared the human body's ability to balance its temperature through homeostasis to Gaia's process of temperature regulation, which illustrates not only Gaia's innate intelligence but also how we humans are a reflection of her. Without this "intelligence network," as Lovelock writes in *Gaia: A New Look at Life on Earth*, "our lifeless Earth, no longer a colorful misfit, a planet that broke all the rules, would fall soberly into line, in barren steady state, between its dead brother and sister, Mars and Venus."

This reflection, each to the other, human and earthly Mother, is echoed in many teachings from the ancient mystical arts. Our ancestors understood many things that we are just now rediscovering through science and metaphysics. Take, for example, the following law of occult doctrine, which was taught and recognized by Renaissance alchemists and Magicians and is still used in Wiccan ritual.

As above, so below;
as the Universe, so the Soul;
as within, so without.

It is said to come from the Emerald Tablet of the ancient Magician and sage, Hermes Trismegistus, who is sometimes deified.

We can see this same principle expressed in how our human bodies, as well as those of other mammals, mirror the balance in temperature and composition that Earth regulates in herself and her atmosphere in order to maintain ideal health.

Of course these are ideal states. By now we all know that human activity has thrown Earth's atmosphere out of balance. One need only think of the so-called Greenhouse Effect, a global warming caused by emissions from burning fossil fuels and other pollutants that have become trapped in Earth's atmosphere. This warming has already caused destructive changes in weather patterns, in the seas, in forests, in animal life, and in humanity. The Greenhouse Effect is, in fact, only one indication among many today that Mother Gaia is ill, and much of her illness is directly caused by human activity. Likewise many illnesses in humans and other species are linked to environmental degradation.

As the Gaia Hypothesis indicates, Gaia is intelligent and aware. She works to balance herself and life on Earth. By tapping in to our deep connection with that intelligence, we can work to heal her. *We can learn to communicate with her—and to develop a deeper communion with her.* We can also communicate with her many representative beings, both on the earth plane and on the astral or metaphysical levels.

It is important to note, too, that Lovelock suggests that *Homo sapiens* may simply be an extension of Gaia's brain. We might be Gaia's memory, her data processing and technological abilities. In *Gaia: A New Look at Life on Earth,* he states:

> Still more important is the implication that the evolution of *Homo sapiens,* with his technological inventiveness and his increasingly subtle communications network, has vastly increased Gaia's range of perception. She is now through us awake and aware of herself. She has seen the reflection of her fair face through the eyes of astronauts and the television cameras of orbiting spacecraft. Our sensations of wonder and pleasure, our capacity for conscious thought and speculation, our restless curiosity and drive are hers to share.

Lovelock suggests that it is not just humans who interreact with Gaia but that there are other highly evolved mammals—the great whales, for instance—who may share in this role as well.

Take time to meditate on these extraordinary ideas. Let Gaia's voice speak to you and move through your consciousness. If indeed we are an extension of Mother Gaia, capable of using our knowledge and technology through her influence and urging, imagine what a peaceful, harmonious world we might create! Perhaps she has called to you already. As you begin to deepen your relationship with the primordial Mother, you will start to feel a completely different connection with the world and all the intricate life-forms around you. Remember: you too came from the jungle, from the desert sands, from the seas, from the mud. Traces of that evolution still flow in your blood, salt your tears, shape your bones.

Scientists now know that the smallest changes in Gaia's atmosphere can affect the weather and the climate, which in turn can affect the seas and the continents across the world. Lovelock points out that we have the perfect percentage of oxygen in our atmosphere—even a small increase would cause fires to break out indiscriminately. Doctors have seen how the tiniest shift in our bodies' chemical makeup through hormonal or endocrinal changes affects our moods, minds, and whole sense of self. Why should we not then accept that "God/Goddess works in mysterious ways," as the old expression goes—subtly, delicately causing change in our world? Too often we do not appreciate or even notice subtleties. We expect huge, explosive, Hollywood-esque results from our actions or thoughts, certainly from anything calling itself "magic." However, this is how the energies of the Universe work—deeply and widely, but quietly.

Think of the soft greens of spring that first creep across the land and the trees, an outward sign that the miracle of rebirth has begun again. At first we see only a slight wash of color, similar to Impressionist painters' opaque watercolors, or gouache, magical evidence that the earth is alive and growing. Someone not attuned to Nature could miss the miracle's first signs altogether. Likewise, if we are not attuned, we may miss opportunities to give back to the earth. Rather than tossing our kitchen scraps into the garbage and having them hauled to the local landfill, for instance, we can choose to compost them into a richly fertilizing gift for the soil. Like the medieval alchemists and Magicians who sought to "transmute" dross metals into gold, those who are aware and attuned to the magic all around us can use composting as a form of pure alchemy in our very own kitchens and gardens.

Wiccan History and Deep Ecology's Forerunners

Modern Wicca has a short modern history with a long and venerable bloodline, as does Deep Ecology. While it is beyond the scope of this book to cover the full history of either, let me offer a few key names and points. We could say that this is a history of those who have, in one form or another, heard Gaia's voice.

Deep Ecology in the United States and Europe sprang from the work of nineteenth- and twentieth-century philosopher-ecologists including Henry David Thoreau, Ralph Waldo Emerson, and Aldo Leopold. These forerunners of the North American ecology movement built on the works of European writers, artists, and poets of the seventeenth, eighteenth, and nineteenth centuries who sensed the sacredness of the web of life and the call of the divine in Nature. In the past thirty years various well-known writers, including Arne Naess, Theodore Roszack, Joanna Macy, and Gary Snyder, to name a very few, have explored the themes of Deep Ecology. The concept of Deep Ecology is usually attributed to Norwegian philosopher Arne Naess, who first discussed it in detail in 1972. He proposed a new realm of study that could be termed *ecosophy,* "a philosophy of ecological harmony or equilibrium."

In this view of humanity's relationship with Nature, we are an integral part of the natural world, sharing a oneness and an equality with all beings; we do not dominate Nature as is generally accepted in the Judeo-Christian tradition. Deep Ecology shares with Wicca and Paganism the idea that Divinity is "immanent"—dwelling in and permeating all of Nature. This philosophy is often called either Pantheism, or Panentheism, depending on one's interpretation of the terms.

Wicca's current form hails only from the early to mid–twentieth century. Unless we include the Victorian period's Renaissance of interest in the occult, the Golden Dawn et alia, it must be considered a recently organized phenomenon incorporating and consolidating many ancient practices. Some have pointed at the medieval Knights Templar, at medieval and Renaissance Free Masonry, and at other more recent influences as background to Wicca's evolution.

This formal religious tradition incorporates the beliefs of many Pagan, pre-Christian, polytheistic Earth religions. The practitioners are part of an Initiatory tradition, a Priest- and Priesshood, and are bound by a code of honor and ethics known as "The Wiccan Rede." Its message is summarized in the commonly quoted admonition: "An [sic] it harm none, do what ye will." This archaic English means: "If you harm no one, you may do as you like." Wiccan traditions generally regard the earth as sacred and as embodying divine spirit, often known as Gaia. It is an *inclusive* religion, as polytheistic Pagan religions generally are, and is still flexible and growing, finding its shape. The modern form is often called "Neo-Paganism," to distinguish it from earlier eras. I will use the simpler term, Paganism.

Many ask, "Are Wicca and Witchcraft the same? What is their connection with Paganism?" The simple answer is that all Wiccans are Witches and Pagans, but not all Witches and Pagans are Wiccans. Paganism in particular is an umbrella term for many polytheistic world traditions, whether you look at the original American Indian tribal religions; the indigenous African, Asian, or South Pacific religions; the ancient classical Mediterranean cultures; the pre-Christian European traditions; or any others. Many people who are not initiated practice spellcraft and various techniques of magic; they can be called Witches, but they are not Wiccan.

In a sense one could say that the two modern paths, Wicca and Deep Ecology, were conceived, gestated, and born in similar times and through similar circumstances, in part through the nascent environmental consciousness and movements of the past two centuries. One might also add the Feminist movement to this fertile era's brainchildren. Indeed there is a connection among the three philosophies and movements. We are witnessing a true renaissance in Earth-revering thought and philosophy, springing forth from many camps. Some who work in these fields use other names for themselves, for example Eco-Pagans or Eco-Feminists; some might call the area of thought Biocentrism or Bio-ethics. However, these are mere labels, nothing more than semantics, like so much of what we humans discuss and debate ad infinitum. What truly matters are our thoughts, emotions, and actions as well as the awareness that our actions, even small acts of conservation or the projection of healing energy, can help to restore Gaia.

The Gaia Group and Other Wiccan Deep Ecologists

Less documented are the more recent traditions of Wicca that teach a kind of enlightened ecology and Earth Stewardship. The phrase *Earth Stewardship* is used by many with an ecological consciousness. In the tradition of Wicca that I practice, the founders define it as "an initiatory Earth religion with Wiccan roots, dedicated to the care and protection of Mother Earth through both magical and practical means." My aim here is to add to the body of literature and the manuals of magical practice related to spiritual Earth Stewardship, not to create another introductory book to Wiccan practices for the Neophyte.

As the environmental movement began to grow and gather momentum in the 1960s and early 1970s, Wiccans also began to wake up to the relationship between the two burgeoning movements and philosophies. In the early 1970s, two young Wiccan leaders living in New York City began to disseminate their ideas on Craft devotion to Mother Earth and the connected concept of our sacred duty as Wiccans. Incredibly, they met with derision and a general lack of interest. Today, with the huge growth in environmental awareness and responsibility in the general public as well as in the Pagan community, such a negative reaction seems incomprehensible.

These two admirable and unpretentious early magical activists are my Initiators and the founders of the Gaia Group. Since they work "regular jobs" and do not feel comfortable fully revealing their Wiccan roles,

I will call them by their public Wiccan community names: Myrddin and Crystal. Crystal recalls from the early 1970s:

> There were a lot of pressures in the political arena at that point. The Vietnam War was finally over. However, the Cold War was in full swing, and most people believed there would be another Vietnam sooner or later. We were still living very much in fear of atomic war. If my memory serves me right, the fear of atomic war was what gave birth to our desire to 'save the planet.' But we soon realized that there was more to saving the planet than averting war. The Gaia Network originally was founded to promote magic for global peace and expanded of its own to include the environment. Neither of us ever sat down and had a full-blown revelation from the Goddess. It all just sort of grew. I think a lot of minds were attuned to the same thing at the same time. I believe that Divine Mother used the threat of atomic war to wake us up.

Crystal has admirable humility about her contributions, as she credits Gaia with moving the Peace Network. Crystal shrugs praise off, saying: "We were just Witches who listened to Momma."

There have always been some in Witchcraft and Paganism who espoused a green consciousness. The much-mourned poet laureate of Wicca, Doreen Valiente (who died in September 1999), wrote of an ecological awareness in the early twentieth century in the U.K. Craft. Avantgarde Pagan and New Age communities and covens, such as the Church of All Worlds (CAW) of the Zells, put forth similar ideas. CAW is still publishing its Pagan environmental journal, *Green Egg*, after some thirty years. In a 1995 edition of *Green Egg* Anodea Judith, a High Priestess with CAW, described their ecological vision: ". . . our Mission Statement: to evolve a network of information, mythology, and experience to awaken the divine within and to provide a context and stimulus for reawakening Gaia and reuniting Her children through tribal community, responsible stewardship, and evolution of consciousness."

Perhaps the best-known activist is Starhawk, the author of some of Paganism and modern Witchcraft's seminal works. Her second work, *Dreaming the Dark* (1982), described in detail her community's extraordinary activist commitment. However, such environmental awareness and commitment was spotty and not much touted by the larger Craft community in the 1960s and early '70s.

The Gaia Group, which formed in 1977, is today a recognized coven and grove of teaching. Myrddin and Crystal were well trained and well connected in the American Wiccan community of the 1970s, when the Craft was rapidly beginning to take shape in the United States. Although they originated in different Wiccan traditions, they shared an enormous compassion and concern for Mother Earth and all her beings. In creating a new tradition, based in "traditional Wicca" but breaking new ground by espousing the path of Earth Stewardship, they broke away from the standard Craft practices of the time.

Crystal has said that their disillusionment with the Craft community was so profound that they considered changing to another tradition of the magical arts and even giving up teaching. Thankfully, they did not. Various synchronicities, such as Starhawk's publication of *Dreaming the Dark,* gave them heart and cheer. They realized they were not alone in their commitment to the earth, to activism, and to magic. Starhawk and her extended coven families, the "Reclaiming Collective" and others, have risked their lives and certainly their freedom with protests and Direct Actions of their own devising. They have many times been arrested and even imprisoned for their actions.[2] As Crystal has said, Starhawk's approach was and is quite different from the Gaia Group's, but the commitment and passion are the same.

Kisma Stepanich, another American author, has also published on an Earth-healing path. One of her books on Paganism is called *The Gaia Tradition,* published in 1991. Her tradition is very different from the Gaia Group's ways of Earth Healing but is a powerful Earth-centered Goddess tradition.

Myrddin and Crystal founded the Gaia Group World Peace Network with the intention of making all magical people aware of the sacredness of Earth and her myriad problems. They also intended to provide a foundation for a worldwide system of ongoing magical workings to help create international peace as well as environmental healing. Today that awareness is something that almost all Wiccan groups pay homage to and many perform active work on. The Gaia Group Network exists as a philosophy and a way of life. It is clear to many of us involved in this work that Gaia is providing the guidance necessary.

I experienced the truly expansive nature of the Gaia Group World Peace Network and of Gaia's voice in the Wiccan community in 1990 when I presented a couple of workshops at a Wiccan Conference in Germany. When I told the group who I was and who my Initiators were, one German man seemed stunned to meet an actual Initiate and member of the Gaia Group (GG). He and his coven had consistently been performing the GG Peace rituals in Germany at the synchronized times of the Global Network suggested by Myrddin and Crystal. Emotions were still running very high in Europe that summer about the end of the Cold War; the Berlin Wall had just come down the previous fall. Today with rituals on the Internet and communications being exchanged so quickly among spiritual communities across the globe, this sort of chance meeting might not seem so remarkable. However, in the 1980s Witches had not started using the Internet and word of the Peace Network had to spread through journals, mailings, or by word of mouth.

The Old Gods had retreated and faded ever deeper into the recesses of the collective unconscious over the past centuries. As people forgot them and neglected them, as Christianity drove people out of the fields and woods, into the cities and the churches, the Gods' and Elementals' power waned. They began to vanish from the earth. A deep truth lies in *Peter Pan:* As Peter says, a fairy dies each time a child says he or she does not believe in fairies.

Vivianne Crowley wrote years ago:

In caverns deep the Old Gods sleep
But the trees still know their Lord.
And it's the Pipes of Pan that play the tune
In the twilight in the wood.
The trees they dance to the Goat God's tune
And they whisper His name to the winds.
And the oak tree dreams of a God with horns
And knows no other King.[3]

Westerners have felt the calling from the Inner Planes, have felt the hunger deep inside for more, have sensed that atavistic call of the Old Religion. A reawakening has begun. As people have once again begun to honor Earth, to revere her beauty as holy, her essence and influence also have grown stronger. She hears us; she responds. In a sense this exemplifies the British Wiccan saying, "The Gods need us as much as we need them."

Deep Ecologists and Earth Stewards can come from different lifestyles, needs, financial commitments, family structures, geographical locations, and cultures, to name a few factors. However, the point is to make *a commitment to conscious and more sustainable living in whatever way we can.*

We must live our magic in order to walk our talk, and vice versa.

To that end, you will find a section called "Gaia Goals" at the end of each chapter, which lists a number of ideas for living out your activism on the practical, mundane level, too. Each small step we take can lead to Deep Ecology, and thus to healing Gaia. All those who love Gaia and her exquisite diversity of life can claim a ministry in her service. As for the importance of working on both the spiritual *and* the mundane levels, I can tell you from experience that many work intently on one level, but not at all on the other. These people miss an essential part of the equation.

Let's move now toward the exercises that will help you become magical activists. I want to start building your magical toolkit by introducing a few techniques that will help you to intensify and heighten your connection with Gaia. The first two exercises are fundamental to all magical work; the third will bring you closer to Gaia.

First Exercises and Skill Building

Before we proceed to the first skills for building your magical toolkit, let's talk a bit about magic. *Magic* is commonly defined as the altering and changing of reality through concentration and will. A Magician or Witch must train his or her will and power of focus in order to put that energy into the Universe clearly and dynamically with the purpose of effecting change in the world. In later chapters, and particularly in chapter 7, we will discuss some of the more advanced concepts behind magic. For now it is sufficient to know that a person who wants to change reality must learn to focus very intently, using deep relaxation, imagination, and visualization.

You might see these first exercises as a means of building a psychic and metaphysical toolkit. In Wicca and Paganism we also have physical tools, such as the magical dagger or sword used in ritual, which I will discuss in later chapters. However, these mental and psychic tools are equally important.

This first exercise is your groundwork, a beginning pathworking, and is ideal for relaxing and accessing the deeper levels of mind. For those not familiar with the term *pathworking*, this is the expression often used in Wicca and Paganism for a type of guided visualization. Like visualization, pathworking is more active than meditation.

Perhaps you're familiar with the concept of shamanic journeying. A pathworking is similar in that it induces a trance state, but it does so by a different method. In shamanic journeying the unconscious is transported to other realms of consciousness by listening to drumming, live or taped. The steady beat of the drum acts as the vehicle. Some shamanic teachers call the drum "the horse" that carries the Shaman or shamanic student. In pathworking, the voice of the leader, together with the images he or she introduces, transport the listener to the trance state and beyond. An experienced visualizer can go into a pathworking without a leader, using a predetermined place or image as a beginning. For this experience, I will act as your leader or guide.

The term *meditation* is bandied around rather loosely these days. Some people use it to avoid the Christian-slanted term, *prayer*. However, the two are not interchangeable. There is an old saying that captures the difference: prayer is talking to God and meditation is listening to the answer. Generally, meditation is still and prayer is active. The first stills the conscious mind, allowing it to hear the inner guidance one receives, from whatever the source. Prayer involves actively asking for answers to desires and needs, from whatever power one believes in.

The ability to relax totally, to focus the mind deeply, and to allow the deeper levels of the mind to take over are essential skills for effective magic and ritual. These abilities are also tools for developing one's connection with the Gods, the Elementals, and the denizens of other planes, such as Angels. I have listed in the recommended reading section several fine books that give techniques on meditation, trance work, visualization, and magic in general. There are also tapes that offer assistance with journeying and pathworking.

The following technique will actually induce a form of *light* trance. We need to have the ability to enter trance for magical or ritual work. Many people resist the trance state out of fear, but there's no need to be afraid. If a fire alarm rings, you will still be alert enough to know to leave the building; if someone tells you to jump out the window or anything else you would not do when fully awake, you will not feel moved to do it. You will not become lost in a trance. I can vouch for this from my work with students and associates for many, many years.

If you are working alone, you may want to tape the visualizations and play them back as you work.

Exercise 1: Preparing for Magic with Deep Relaxation

Get into a comfortable position, either sitting or lying down. Close your eyes. Begin to let all tension go from your body. Work your way up through your body, muscle by muscle, organ by organ, limb by limb. Visualize each one relaxing; speak to each muscle or organ mentally at first if it helps. ("I feel my feet relax, now my knees. My leg muscles have become loose and easy.") Feel the relaxation creep through you. Know that you are safe and that you have nowhere else you need to be. There is nothing else you have to do right this minute. This is where you need to be. Your muscles have no task now except to relax, to soften and sink into the earth.

As you feel relaxation growing and your body getting heavier, notice the day's tension slip away. You are alert and aware, but deeply, deeply relaxed. Let your mind flow, freely. See what images or messages come to you. Give yourself permission to relax into this level of consciousness. It is a source of healing power and inspiration.

In your own time and at your own pace, gently come back to your surroundings from deep relaxation.

I will refer back to this exercise in the later pathworkings and magical workings, so it is important to practice it often and learn to do it very effectively.

Another exercise that I consider fundamental to magic involves connecting with the energy around you and learning to use your body as a channel for that energy. You can also use it to cast a protective shield around yourself, which can be useful for simply living in our often precarious world and for preparing for acts of magic or ritual. I use this exercise with all kinds of people—beginning Wiccan students, adults whom I counsel who are not practiced in the magical arts or meditation, and others. It is also a good exercise for children.

As we will see in later chapters, protection is *essential,* at all times, in magic and in ritual practice. We are vulnerable to outside influences that come into our consciousness and affect the health of our mind, body, and spirit. Whether at home, out in the world, or in the Magic Circle, we can leave ourselves open to what has sometimes been termed "psychic attack." This second exercise goes hand in hand with the first; as we open ourselves through relaxation, we can become more vulnerable. We will talk about this in detail in later chapters and exercises. There are many ways to create a protective shield for ourselves, and here is a good way to begin. Whatever your background and training, this is an essential part of your visualization toolkit. In later exercises when I ask you to "connect and protect," come back to this exercise.

Exercise 2: Connection and Protection

Begin with the relaxation technique detailed above. Or, if you are continuing on from exercise 1, maintain your deep relaxation.

Bring your awareness to the base of your spine. Imagine a current of energy that extends from the earth to the base of your spine. This energy from Gaia comes up to meet you each time you inhale. It is a sparkling green.

As you breathe, gently and rhythmically, visualize that current of warm, nourishing Earth energy rising up to you. It meets and enters your body at the spine, where there is a red light. See the red light as a kind of window through which the Gaia energy can enter. Gaia's green light moves up along your spine, through your whole body. Feel it soothe and revitalize you as it flows.

The energy reaches the crown of your head, where you see a window or opening of beautiful, sparkling white light. The Gaia energy now flows out through the portal at the crown of your skull.

As you breathe, become aware of the energy that reaches down to you from the heavens. This celestial white light flows down from the stars and the cosmos. It enters the very top of your head, through the window at your crown, and courses down your spine. The glowing, sparkling white energy meets with the brilliant green light at about the area of your navel, or solar plexus.

The two energies mix within you, pleasantly and warmly. They connect you to both of your birthrights—the earth and the stars. You are a child of both, of the earth and of the cosmos . . . Mother Earth and Father Sky. Your body has become a channel for Divine energy, which is always there to nourish, heal, and protect you. You are also a channel for the intermingling of the two energy sources, earthly and celestial. This energy is holy as you are holy. It is of the Divine, as you are and as Nature is. Remember that it is a natural part of who you are and a natural part of your own energy field. You can always "plug in" to these power sources, to be revitalized, soothed, protected. They are there for you, as for all of us.

The two energy currents mix at your center and continue on their paths, up and down. The current from the earth continues to flow up your spine and spills out the top of your head. As it leaves your crown, it transforms into glowing white energy that cascades over you in a shower of cosmic light. As that light surrounds and envelopes you, you are protected by a shield of Divine love and power. See that egg of light encasing you and protecting you.

In this way you can always connect to Divine protection and to the power of the cosmos. Remember this feeling and this visualization. Recall that you have a bright red portal at the base of your spine that receives and gives out Earth energy. At the top of your head the portal allows cosmic, celestial energy to flow in and out. Those two lovely lights should always glow brightly, red and white. Visualize them often.

Let your breathing quietly continue to bring the energies into you for a few more minutes. Then in your own time, let your awareness come back from deep relaxation to normal consciousness.

Practice connecting and protecting often, until you can do it immediately and instantaneously, until it becomes so second nature that you can visualize those energy fields with your eyes open, for example while walking down the street or driving your car. Practice seeing that oval-shaped white light of protection encircling other things besides yourself: around your bed, around your car, around your loved ones.

Later, if you choose to, you can learn about visualizing and casting the full Wiccan-style Magic Circle of Power for complete ritual workings.

In the final exercise of this chapter, we'll practice a technique for surrounding anyone or anything with forms of energy. This technique is used by many traditions and religions, those under the umbrella of New Age as well as other diverse paths, including Wicca. However, it is fundamentally a magical technique. This very important and effective method allows you to send healing and protection quickly to those you care about. As you will see, we will use this technique to send healing energy to our Mother Planet. We have learned how to relax deeply to begin magical practice and to create a basic shield of protection. Now we will take the first step in projecting and shaping energy—the true basis of magical technique.

Exercise 3: Meeting Gaia

*Return to the relaxed state that you learned in exercise 1 and start to visu-
alize our beautiful Mother Planet.*

Imagine that you are gently flying away from Earth's surface, away
from the place where you are sitting or lying. You are flying out of Earth's
atmosphere. You are like an astronaut, but you don't need a space suit.
You can fly here and there, drifting happily in the rarified gas of space.

From space, floating, turning slowly, you can see Earth. It looks like
the pictures or posters you have seen taken from space. There is Gaia,
in all her beauty and glory . . . a blue-green gem sparkling amid the
heavens. Take a moment to focus on our planet, to take in all her wonder and loveliness. She is our source of life and energy; she is the vehicle on which we ride to our greater destiny, our foremost and most intimate companion in the galaxy. Mother. Source.

See the protective layers surrounding Gaia, the protective covering
we breathe and live in daily, unaware of its blessings. Look at the seas
and oceans. See how they predominate, more blue/green/turquoise
watery realms than gray/brown/red/green landforms. However each
continent has its own distinguishing colors. Can you tell which continent is which? See if you can identify the mountain ranges, deserts, rain-
forests, and curves of the landmasses. Perhaps you can make out the
Great Wall of China or the Great Pyramids of Egypt, some of the only
human-made structures visible at this distance. Do they remind you of
our human efforts to control our environment? Look at the colors and
the forms and the ever-changing face of our planet.

In your mind and your heart, say hello to Gaia. Greet her in a gracious and courteous way, as you would an honored new friend. Or if you
are already in a communication with Gaia, then greet her as you would
an honored family member or old friend. Commune with her for a
moment.

Remember that Gaia is alive. She can feel your thoughts and your
feelings. You send energy out when you think or feel something. Your
thoughts and emotions change the energy field around your body, and
perceptive beings of all kinds can perceive that change. Gaia can feel the
thoughts you project to her. So, now, in your own way, project love and
gratitude to Gaia. Let her know how you appreciate all she does, and has
done for eons, for life on Earth.

If it helps you to visualize the energy you send as a color, then see in your mind's eye a current of pink light going out to her. Watch as it surrounds her with a ball of pink light—that is your love surrounding her. Pink is often seen as the "color frequency" of love and compassion. Focus on that visualization for a few moments.

Next you will send healing thoughts and energy to Gaia. If you'd like, think of specific things that symbolize healing to you. For example, see the oceans sparkling with life and light—fish jumping, dolphins surfacing, birds flying over the seas in flocks. Or visualize a forest full and green, teeming with life of every kind.

If you find the concept of colors easier, then send Gaia another current of colored energy, this time in blue. See Gaia enveloped in soothing, rich tones of azure energy, the color frequency of healing. Blue is one of the healing tones and currents of the universe. Blue is also the color of the first kind of magical energy Wiccans and Magicians see, that of etheric energy. You can use this kind of visualization anytime you want to send healing energy—whether to our Mother Planet or to some other being.

Slowly, when you are ready, bid farewell to Gaia for now—although you are never really far from her, of course. Will yourself to gently float back down toward Earth's surface. Down you come toward the blue-green ball of diverse life that you call home. Float back to where you originated, your room, your favorite place in Nature, wherever. And slowly return to awareness of your space.

With these three exercises, you have truly begun on the path of developing a psychic toolkit. You also have begun learning how to use time-honored magical techniques for the purpose of practicing magical Deep Ecology.

A Beloved Ode

Now that we have "met" Gaia, and begun the techniques of centering ourselves for meditation, pathworking, and magic, I want to close this chapter by introducing the Charge of the Goddess, a part of the Wiccan body of literature used worldwide as a meditational or inspirational tool.

The history of this beautiful and moving piece has been theorized by many. In short, it was both taken by Doreen Valiente and Gerald Gardner from various sources and written by them. Some sections were adapted from Charles Leland's *Aradia: The Gospel of the Witches,* which documented the practices of Tuscan Witches who kept alive the ancient religion of "Stregheria," or traditional Italian Witchcraft. Sections were written by Doreen Valiente, and some wording was adapted from Aleister Crowley.

However, its true origins, line by line, may never be completely traced. And perhaps the origins are not as important as the fact that the Charge has become a beloved and much-honored part of Wiccan ritual. The Charge of the Goddess forms a fundamental part of the Wiccan Book of Shadows and is used by many Wiccans in ritual as the teachings or "holy word" of the Goddess. Although it is a Mystery Tradition of ancient heritage, Wicca has no holy book like the Bible, Talmud, or the Koran. We draw from the ancient spiritual teachings of many societies, and many of those traditions were originally oral traditions. Or, sadly, many of the existing ancient texts were destroyed. However, the Wiccan Rede ("An it harm none, do what ye will") and the Charge of the Goddess are two pieces that might be said to form the core of Wiccan "dogma," if I dare to use the word.

The Charge is one of the few pieces that could truly stand as Wiccan Credo. I consider it an inspired sacred text, like the holy books of other world religions. I have seen the tangible power it brings forth, even when recited in a classroom under fluorescent lights. The first time I read the Charge (from a Wiccan calendar, while standing casually in a New York City bookstore), I felt as if a bolt of lightning had hit me. Reading the Charge was part of the spiritual epiphany that led me to Wicca.

This is not word for word from the original version. I have adapted it slightly for my coven's ritual work from the Gaia Group's Book of Shadows and from other sources. However, it is largely the same. The recitation of the Charge may be carried out by Priests and Priestesses inside the Sacred Circle according to the tradition and manner deemed appropriate by the coven. It may be used as a part of the powerful practice known as "Drawing Down the Moon," or it may be used simply as a tool for meditation or prayer. (The practices used in the Wiccan Circle, such as Drawing Down the Moon, are discussed in appendix B, which gives the full Circle Casting.)

In whatever circumstance and whatever location I call the Charge to mind, I find it instantly calming and centering.

If you have never encountered the Charge of the Goddess before, take time to contemplate the imagery it offers. It is a powerful ode to the divine feminine energy of our world. Let the experience of visualizing our Earth in all her magnificence meld now with the poetry of this beloved piece.

The Charge of the Goddess

Listen to the words of the Great Mother, She who was of old also called among men Artemis, Astarte, Athene, Dione, Melusine, Aphrodite, Cerridwen, Diana, Arianrhod, Isis, Bride, and by many other names.

Whenever ye have need of anything, once in the month and better it be when the Moon is full, then shall ye assemble in some secret place and adore the spirit of me, who am Queen of all the Witches.

There shall ye assemble, ye who are feign to learn all sorcery, yet have not won my deepest secrets. To these will I teach things that are yet unknown.

And ye shall be free from slavery, and as a sign that ye be really free, ye shall be naked in your rites, and ye shall dance, sing, feast, make music and love, all in my praise.

For mine is the ecstasy of the spirit and mine also is joy on Earth; for my law is love unto all beings. Keep pure your highest ideals; strive ever toward them. Let naught stop you nor turn you aside. For mine is the secret door that opens upon the Land of Youth, and mine is the cup of the wine of life, and the Cauldron of Cerridwen, which is the Holy Grail of immortality.

I am the gracious Goddess who gives the gift of joy unto the heart of man. Upon Earth I give knowledge of the spirit eternal; and beyond death, I give peace and freedom and reunion with those who have gone before. Nor do I demand sacrifice, for behold, I am the Mother of all living and my love is poured out upon the earth.

Hear ye the words of the Star Goddess, She in the dust of whose feet are the hosts of heaven and whose body encircleth the universe.

I who am the beauty of the green Earth, and the white Moon among the stars, and the mystery of the waters, and the desire of the heart of man, I call unto thy soul to arise and come unto me. For I am the soul of nature, who giveth life to the universe. From me all things proceed, and unto me all things must return. Before my face, beloved of the Gods and of men, let thine innermost divine self be enfolded in the raptures of the infinite.

Let my worship be in the heart that rejoiceth. For behold, all acts of love and pleasure are my rituals. Therefore let there be beauty and strength, power and compassion, honor and humility, mirth and reverence within thee.

And thou who thinkest to seek for me, know that thy seeking and yearning shall avail thee not unless thou knowest the mystery:

If that which thou seekest, thou findest it not within thee, thou wilt never find it without thee. For behold, I have been with thee from the beginning and I am that which is attained at the end of desire.

Remember, the Charge was written at various time periods and by various people. It is not taken literally by everyone who uses it in ritual or in Wicca. I encourage you to interpret it according to your own beliefs and inner guidance, as you would with any inspirational text. For example, reference to being "naked in their rites" may well have been inserted by Gerald Gardner, who was a naturist or nudist. Some Wiccans believe in doing magic "skyclad," others do not, preferring to perform their rites in specially designed ritual robes, or even in everyday clothes. It is a very individual choice.

What is most important here is to remember that you are entering into a new relationship, or a new level of relationship, with the magnificent, loving being called Gaia and that the Charge will help you communicate with her. Practice the visualizations given above as you grow in relationship. This innately intelligent force that balances our planet, which James Lovelock recognized by her Goddess name, Gaia, needs you. She needs your love and healing. In return, as you open your intuition and your heart to her, her power and her inspiration will touch you. The healing and love that you send to her will return back to you. You can experience a miraculous loop of healing energy, from which all can benefit. You've truly begun on the path of Gaian magic.

❀❀❀❀❀❀❀❀

Gaia Goals

❀ Fit more conservation into every aspect of your life: Reuse, Recycle, Reduce!

❀ Use it up, wear it out, make it do—resist consumerism; repair and reuse what you can.

❀ Recycle whatever you can—buy used clothes and household things; recycle your paper, plastics, metals, and so on.

❀ Find out how to conserve resources in your home more efficiently—adapt your heating, electricity, water use; install better insulation; and so on.

❀ Get out of your car! Better yet, get rid of your car if you can. Ride a bike, use mass transit, carpool.

❀ Buy a hybrid-powered vehicle (combination combustion and electric powered) or one that runs on greener fuels.

❀ If you are working in construction or renovating, use recycled timber and other sustainable materials wherever possible. Practice sustainable building techniques in every way that you can.

❀ Make space in your life for stillness. In that stillness you will begin to hear Gaia's voice and the voice of life around you.

Chapter 2
Lessons in Balance and Simplicity

All things in Nature are in balance,
All wholes are composed of their parts
In harmonious balance.

From the Gaia Group Book of Shadows

People come to Earth Spirituality today for many reasons. Some seek answers through magic and ritual. Some hope for an intoxicating mystical experience that they have sensed in Nature. Some seek the Divine Feminine, lost in much of Christianity, Judaism, and Islam. Of course, there are movements within these traditional, mainstream religions that honor Earth and the Divine Feminine, and that advocate environmentalism. Among them, as mentioned earlier, is Creation Spirituality, a mystical Earth-centered tradition of Christianity made known by Matthew Fox. Unitarian Universalism is a modern religious movement that draws from not only Judeo-Christian roots, but also from the world's indigenous and Pagan Earth-honoring traditions.

Paganism, Wicca, and other Earth religions can offer all of the beneficial aspects listed above. For many seekers, however, it is not only magic, ritual, the Divine Feminine, or the concept of immanence that they want from the Earth religions. It is also the vital sexuality and sensuality that draws them, a spirituality that honors the body, its senses, and physical pleasures. Respecting human sexuality is a time-honored aspect of Paganism, linked often to the ecstatic, Dionysian side of the Ancient Mysteries. For some, Paganism offers a release from inhibition, an escape from Judeo-Christian society's repressiveness and childhood shackles. For others it represents a denial of society's conformist mores or rebellion in midlife. Some may be seeking outlets in artistic self-expression: they revel in elaborate costume making, for example, as seen in those who flock to Renaissance Fairs and Witches' Balls or to the "Society for Creative Anachronism" conventions. There are Pagans and Wiccans who find self-expression in *Star Trek* and *Star Wars* conventions and the costumes worn there.

All of these ways of expressing ourselves, of freeing our bodies for sexual and sensual play, provided they "harm none," are, according to the Earth religions, good and right. In fact we would say that having fun should be a regular part of our lives and our rituals. If nothing else, it can sustain us and help to prevent the psychic and emotional burnout that is so common among activists.

Perhaps you're familiar with the expression "Follow your bliss," which has been attributed to the great writer on mythology Joseph Campbell. From a Wiccan perspective, bliss is an intimate aspect of divinity, of the ineffable experience of the sacred. It revitalizes us. Furthermore, reclaiming the beauty and the sacred in the human body ultimately has a balancing effect on the larger society. Philosophies that teach disdain and unloving attitudes toward the body and the material world feed violence and unhealthy mores, sexual and otherwise. Repression has been shown over and over to give rise to explosive and occasionally destructive rebellion as the pendulum swings to the other extreme. Recognizing the joyousness connected with the divine leads us to the miraculous loop that we participate in when we work in Gaian magic. Nature is surging with primal, sensual energies, not only in spring or summer but at all times, and by following your bliss you can tap in to these energy sources. This primal vitality of Nature has been sym-bolized throughout history by randy, exuberant Earth, Forest, and Vineyard Gods, including Pan, Bacchus, Silenus, and Dionysus.

This joyous, blissful, and sometimes erotic connection with Nature is healthy and right. It can lead us back to a rightful reclaiming of what some writers and psychologists call our "authentic" self or even our wild self. What we call "civilization" has many necessary calming and social-izing effects on human nature, of course, and has led humanity to cre-ate some beautiful cities, cultural centers, and so on. However, there are degrees and degrees, as in all things. Some aspects of the socialization process are necessary for a society to function. And some aspects of that process, which we all go through as children to one extent or another, can rob of us of our connection with the genuine nature residing in our deepest and most ancient selves. In the hidden corners of our minds and psyches reside essential truths and instincts and healthy sources of aware-ness. As the inspiring Buddhist Deep Ecologist and poet Gary Snyder wrote: "Civilization is part of nature—our egos play in the fields of the unconscious—history takes place in the Holocene—human culture is rooted in the primitive and the paleolithic—our body is a vertebrate mammal being—and our souls are out in the wilderness."

Our souls *are* out in the wilderness, indeed. Haven't you ever marveled at the imagery in your dreams and how your unconscious mind can incorporate such surprisingly vivid and primal images? The more authentic we can let ourselves be, the healthier we will be. To quote another well-known adage, this one from Shakespeare: "To thine own self be true."

Yet, as the ancient Greeks taught, one must seek moderation in all things. Just as in the hedonistic period toward the decline of the Roman Empire, ecstatic revelry and self-indulgent sensuality can sometimes be little more than "fiddling while Rome burns." If our spirituality means nothing more than fun and escapism, there is little point to calling ourselves Pagans, Wiccans, or Earth Magicians.

As a spiritual path and practice, Wicca and Paganism offer a means to personal evolution—spiritual, emotional, and psychological—through a reclaiming of balance in all: between yin and yang, male and female, darkness and light. This also includes the balance between the quietly reverent and the ecstatically blissful. We cannot be truly healthy as individuals nor as a society without this balance. When the pendulum swings too far in one direction or the other, balance and harmonious right relationships are lost.

Balanced Spirituality to Heal Gaia and Ourselves

This balance affects how we carry out our rituals as well. In my tradition, we are expected to keep Earth Healing a constant focus. The goal and the ideal is that every ritual should include some act of Earth Healing, however small or large.

We see the importance of both Low and High Magic. High Magic can be seen as magic that has a higher, loftier purpose, aimed at bettering one's spiritual evolution and of connecting with the Divinity. Such magic might also, in some definitions, involve working with or in service to the greater community. For example, ceremonies that perform acts of healing, or of sending magical energy to protect an ancient forest or other natural site, or simply of communing more closely with a certain aspect of the Gods and Goddesses, in some definitions could be seen as High Magic. Low Magic is more "mundane," perhaps relating to magic such as prosperity spells or love spells. High Magic keeps the practitioner directed toward his or her relationship with the Divinity, while possibly working for a larger goal than the merely personal.

There are other elements that usually differentiate High Magic from Low Magic for a Wiccan—distinctions such as how elaborate and elegant the ceremony is. High Magic rituals can be much lengthier and more formal than Low Magic; they may also involve other occult traditions' magical practices, such as those associated with the Order of the Golden Dawn. Low Magic is thought of as more casual, done more informally, and for this reason is sometimes called "Kitchen Witchery" or "Hedge Witchery" (which is in no way meant as demeaning to the healing work and magic done by such Witches). Whatever the moniker, a truly holistic religious practice should combine the two aims: working with the Divinity, in pursuit of spiritual betterment and in service to the larger community.

At every Temple of Gaia and Gaia Group (GG) ritual we call upon the Divinity to aid us in our rite and in our magical intention. That intention may be to clean up a toxic waste dumping site, to cleanse a river, or to help a friend who is struggling with cancer. Therefore, in essence, we channel a higher power into our work, and we direct our intentions toward our earthly community. This is a holistic spiritual practice, a healthy and balanced spirituality combining High and Low Magic.

Some use the distinctions of Thaumaturgy (Low Magic) versus Theurgy (High Magic). This is quite an arcane discussion and one that requires much more detail than a scant definition. In brief, however, the concepts are defined as:

Thaumaturgy (from Greek *thauma,* wonder or miracle + *ergon,* work; *thaumatourgia,* the supposed working of miracles or magic) Spellmaking that has the aim of bringing about changes in reality as we know it, or even to cause what are commonly seen as "miracles."

Theurgy (from the Greek, *theos,* god + *ergon,* work) Magic and/or spellcraft whose aim is to help the practitioner grow in his or her relationship with Divinity, in whatever aspect he or she has chosen to emulate and to know intimately; this kind of practice brings about positive changes and can accelerate one's spiritual evolution.

Now that we have discussed some of the traditional concepts behind magic, let's continue building the magical toolkit. We have begun to connect with Gaia and with the world around us. Now let's deepen that relationship through more groundwork in heightened awareness.

Exercise 4: Sense Awareness

This exercise invites you to go into Nature and to relax your body com-
pletely. Open up your senses to all that is around, as intimately and as
carefully as you can. Lie on the ground, if you can, or sit under a tree with
your back against its trunk. Do the relaxation process you learned in exer-
cise 1. When you are centered and relaxed, begin.

Keep your eyes closed. Feel the connection with the earth around
you growing. Listen with every fiber of your being. Feel. Smell. Sense it
all. Take it in.

Sense the earth's energy under you, around you. Does it feel like a
person's would, if someone were lying beside you? Do you feel any messages coming into your mind? Do you have a sense of companionship
with the tree near you, the rock, the birds over head, the ants or other
small creatures below you? Let your sense of interconnectedness grow.

Know that your cells, your innermost mysterious, microscopic
makeup, is of the same material as the earth below you . . . Nature around
you. Your lungs need the air blowing around you. Your skin and vital
organs need the moisture in the clouds above you, or the water deep
under the ground. Own that realization. Know it intrinsically.

Feel yourself begin to meld with Gaia. She is your Mother. You are
safe. It is all right to do that.

Live in that sensation for a little while.

When you are ready, bring your awareness back to the physical place
where you are sitting or lying. Do so slowly, but hold some of that
increased awareness still with you. You may begin to feel some of that
heady joyousness mentioned earlier, as the primal energies of Nature
begin to flow through your own energy centers. It is healthy. Let that joy-
fulness or playfulness stay with you. Remember: self-healing is a part of
your experience, too.

Sacrifice as Way toward Balance

Another practice that "fine-tunes" the practitioner to the energies of the
earth involves the concept of sacrifice. This may seem like a departure
from the kind of magic and healing work we've discussed so far but, as
you will soon see, sacrifice is a part of the yin and yang, the giving and
receiving, the balance.

The ancients believed that one must propitiate the Gods with blood sacrifices, and some polytheistic indigenous religions in Africa, Asia, and South America still practice animal sacrifice. Occasionally these ancient customs and beliefs intermingle with Christian ceremonies, such as in the religions of Voodoo, Santeria, and others.

Modern Wicca keeps the memory of ritual sacrifice alive through symbols or with "psycho dramas," short ceremonial plays that sometimes enact symbolic sacrifices. We leave offerings of food and drink, such as ale or wine and bread or cakes, known as "libations," for the Gods and Elementals.

For instance, the ancient society of the British Isles believed that the king had a sacred bond to the land that required his blood to be spilled every few years. This sacrifice renewed the fertility of the land and was his divine royal duty. The last recorded occurrence of this kingly sacrifice took place on August 2, 1100, in England's New Forest with the death of King William II, also known as William Rufus. A stone in the New Forest area still marks the spot. These days, at Lammas or Lughnasadh, the Wiccan High Festival celebrated on August 1, we commemorate this sacrifice with a ritual drama, where a Priest acts the part of the Sacrificial King, often called the Corn King. Participants also frequently think of something they can offer from their lives, a personal sacrifice that they may give to the Gods.

In the GG, we follow the concept of "I sacrifice myself to myself." This means that we consider our actions in the light of the greater good. To many Americans, this will sound repressive or strange. Sacrifice has certainly fallen out of favor. However, seeing our actions in a wider context is good for our souls and good for the earth. We might not pour blood on the earth as in ancient practice, but perhaps choose instead to shun the rampant materialism and consumerism that has gripped our culture in the twentieth and twenty-first centuries. (In the United States alone, per capita consumption grew 45 percent from 1981 to 2001.)

Indeed it might feel like a bloodletting to forego a new car, or perhaps a bigger car like an SUV, to resist buying a larger house, or maybe bearing a third child. We must ask ourselves over and over: "Do I really need that?" "Is the old one I have at home still useful?" "Can I repair it or paint it or somehow clean it up to make it work for me awhile longer?" "Why would I have another child? Do I want to add to the population burdens the earth is already suffering?" The old motto from the Depression and the World War II era—"Use it up, wear it out, make it do"—could return to vogue today as a form of sacrificing oneself to oneself.

Every great spiritual teacher and leader of history—Jesus, Lao-tzu, Confucius, Buddha, Mohammed, Francis of Assisi, Gandhi, Mother Teresa, the list goes on—has advocated renouncing material wealth and the obsessive fixation on possessions. Our ancestors in the original American colonies rebelled against the excesses of the royals as well as the cruelty of the nondemocratic systems of the Old World, and much of the world later followed that lead. If we return to the rich tradition of American thinker Henry David Thoreau, we find in his essay on economy in the time-honored classic *Walden* (1854): "Most of the luxuries, and many of the so-called comforts of life, are not only not indispensable, but positive hindrances to the elevation of mankind. With respect to luxuries and comforts, the wisest have ever lived a more simple and meager life than the poor. The ancient philosophers, Chinese, Hindu, Persian and Greek, were a class which none has been poorer in outward riches, none so rich in inward."

To draw on Thoreau but in an Earth Magician context, a focus on things and on material comforts will ultimately sap our power. We cannot be Deep Ecologists, be committed to healing Gaia, and yet be obsessed with "the mania of owning things" to quote another American visionary, Walt Whitman.

The following early American Shaker hymn, which many religions and organizations, including the Unitarian Universalists, still sing today, says:

'Tis a gift to be simple, 'tis a gift to be free,
'Tis a gift to come down where we ought to be.
And when we find ourselves in the place just right,
'Twill be in the valley of love and delight.

The idea that consumerism will bring peace of heart is a chimera that we chase futilely. Even though we run hard in pursuit of this illusion, we will still be left empty, with souls aching like an empty stomach. Simplicity can lead one into that "place just right." It is healthy and soul restoring. It offers us a means to grow internally, to evolve spiritually. Whoever coined the expression that the environmental movement picked up years ago had the right idea: "Live simply that others may simply live."

Balance and Right Relationship

Our ancient Pagan forebears practiced methods of sacrifice to honor and propitiate the Gods. They also practiced rites that allowed for ecstatic, sensual revelry. They knew that both sides of the whole are necessary for health and balance. Classical Paganism also teaches the concept of "Moderation in All." Like the ancient symbol of yin/yang, Wicca honors the light and the dark, the duality in Nature, and the polarity in energy throughout the Universe.

Our spiritual practice plus divinely aided activism will help to turn back the tide of consumption. It will begin little by little to re-create in human consciousness the ancient paradigm of living in harmony with the earth and the Old Ones. The Voluntary Simplicity movement, which sprang up in the United States in the 1990s, offers us an encouraging sign that people are discovering the value of sacrifice and simplicity. Nature and life-honoring traditions, such as Buddhism and the Native American paths, teach a beautiful thought, "right relationship." Whatever words you choose, harmony, balance, and moderation are the essentials here.

Exercise 5: What Can I Release to Gaia?

Earth is receptive and helpful to us in ways we might never imagine. She takes on our emotions and our garbage, and she tries to break them down and neutralize them. Now we will focus for a few moments on something we can relinquish for own health and betterment, and for the health and betterment of Gaia. We will give it to her to do what is right. Perhaps whatever this is it will come back in another, healthier form . . . rather like the alchemical transmuting of garbage into lovely, soil-restoring compost we mentioned earlier. That is a metaphor we will return to various times.

Begin with a relaxation exercise, then continue:

What do you feel is unnecessary in your life? Is there something that you know you should let go? Have you had trouble doing so?

Perhaps you have a habit that you know is unhealthy, or a part of your diet or daily routine needs to change. Do you want to give up smoking? To start exercising again? Get out of the car and walk more each day? Should you try to become a little more conscious about your diet—maybe give up dessert some nights, or let go of coffee? Become vegetarian, or at least stop eating red meat?

Or do you need to release things? Do you need to get rid of some old clothes? *Stuff* that has accumulated in your home for no good reason? Think on these ideas for a little while.

When you have focused on what you would like to release, see if you can think of it as a gift to Gaia. If you are breaking a habit that's bad for your health, consider that becoming healthier connects your own health with hers. And an effective Earth Steward and Earth Magician needs to be physically healthy—"As above, so below." We must clean up our whole selves in order to be a clear channel for magical power. This ties in to the concept of "Magical Hygiene," which we will discuss in depth later.

If your release has to do with letting go of certain material things, try to find a way to recycle them or allow others to put them to use. Charity bins, garage sales, used-clothing stores, shelters, churches—there are many ways you can put your unwanted things to good use by someone in need.

When you have decided what you will offer in sacrifice, see it in your mind's eye. Wrap it in white light, or blue light—whichever comes more easily to you—and send it into the air. See it floating gently into the sky . . . perhaps it will even slowly vanish as you watch. It has become a gift of sacrifice to Gaia. And you, as a Magician who works on both the physical and magical levels, must act on your promise of sacrifice.

In your own time, come out of deep relaxation.

Creating Blessings and the Sacred

We can choose to create sacred space anywhere. Author and mathematician Michael Schneider, in *A Beginner's Guide to Constructing the Universe,* emphasizes how we bring the sacred with us: "Sacred space is within us. Not in our bodies or brain cells but in the volume of our consciousness. Wherever we go we bring the sacred within us to the sacred around us. We consecrate locations and studies by the presence of this awareness, not just the other way around. . . . Awareness is the ultimate sacred wonder."

We can't buy sacred space; we won't find that kind of awareness in any store or catalog. As you develop your ability to hear Gaia's voice and your skills as a magical Deep Ecologist, you can learn to quietly and subtly spread blessings and balance.

The following exercise blesses our space, linking the sacred with the mundane, practical ecology with Deep Ecology. It also helps to deepen our awareness and mindfulness and to bring that sacred awareness into our surroundings through the elements.

Exercise 6: Balancing Our Own Habitat

As a way of living our determination to help heal Gaia and deepening our commitment to her, let's initiate an exercise in balance in our own space. You can enhance or create this balance in your garden or backyard. If you don't have either available to you, perhaps you can find space nearby to work in—a communal garden area or a bit of land at a friend's or relative's house. If you live in a city and don't have access to a communal garden, you may be able to find a corner of a park or an empty lot to beautify. Perhaps you can simply create a lovely window box garden or a container garden on a fire escape or windowsill, provided it's safe and legal. If all else fails, you can do this as a mental or astral exercise.

Focus on the natural aspect in the place you have chosen to honor, to beautify, or to envision. How could you make this a truly balanced habitat for animals, for wildlife, and for the Nature spirits, the Elementals, or Devas? (See chapter 4 for an in-depth discussion of the Elementals and further exercises on honoring the Nature spirits.)

Think about how planting flowers, trees, plants, or shrubs would offer shade and cover for animals, birds, butterflies. These might also be a good food source or nesting area. And of course, a source of water is essential—a little pond, a bird bath, a large container, whatever form seems best.

Now think of the four elements—earth, air, fire, water—and how they are present or represented in this area. We need them all in our lives; they are an intrinsic part of our earthly makeup. (In a later exercise, we look at how the elements can become balanced in our own personalities.) Let's examine the physical manifestations of the four elements as they grace this natural environment.

Earth is obvious. The land you're working, the flowers or trees or shrubs you're cultivating—all of these are of the element earth. Think about how you can foster the earth's health here, by adding nutrients to the soil, by contributing to the habitat for animals and insects. Beautifying a place with a garden or grove makes a lovely contribution to humans, too, of course! However, the purpose here is to link with Gaia in practical, physical ways.

Air also is obvious. The breezes that move through this area are part of the element of air. By planting green things you enhance the health of this element. Plants help cleanse the air by taking in carbon dioxide, which we produce in too great amounts, and giving off the very oxygen we need to breathe. Here is another example of one of Nature's perfect exchanges.

Fire is harder to incorporate. Perhaps you are working in your back-yard where you hold barbecues. In that sense you bring in the element of fire. Or perhaps you live in an area where you can burn leaves or gar-den clippings in bonfires. If not, you can incorporate the fire element by sprinkling ashes from a fire or burnt incense on the garden to pro-vide extra nutrients to the soil and to bring in the balancing effects of the element of fire.

Please do be careful if you choose to start a fire. Whether on land you own, or in a campsite in a National or State Park, use extreme cau-tion. While fire is an essential part of every ecosystem and has benefi-cial effects, it can easily get out of control. Even the Forest Service has learned that lesson when setting "controlled" fires to burn underbrush; if the brush is very dry, the fire can quickly spread out of control. If you are doing this exercise as a visualization, simply visualize the fire and know that your passion for helping Gaia is a psychological/emotional/spiritual connection with the element of fire.

Water is easier to incorporate into your balanced habitat. It comes in the form of precipitation, as rain or snow. It comes with morning mists and dews; it also comes when you water your garden or new plants. And as we said earlier, birds and small animals appreciate a vessel hold-ing water for them to drink or bathe in. In dry climates, such as where I live, it is especially helpful for them. Water is a precious substance that makes this planet a unique environment in all the cosmos. Water is a magical elixir of life all unto itself.

Now that you have visualized or actually worked in balancing the elements in your natural space, spend a few moments meditating on the effects of that balance. Experience the gifts of each element, both in the environment around you, and in your being. Remember: you are a Deep Ecologist and are therefore connected to Gaia. You are connected to the results of balancing these elements intrinsically within yourself.

Clearly this is an ongoing exercise that you will grow and live with for some time—perhaps for years! Planting a garden, adding plants to a natural space, and creating a balanced habitat is truly finding the sacred on the earth plane. It is one of the greatest satisfactions one can find in a simple form—an act of love, generosity, and creativity as well as a magical act. If you have carried this exercise out as a visualization, you, too, are balancing the elements in your life and are connecting more deeply with them.

Pay attention. If you have wished for a garden or green space of your own, an opportunity may suddenly arise. This is how magic works. Focus, visualization, and clarity of purpose all fuel our magical intentions and help to make the intention reality. We will return to these concepts later.

By creating a balanced space and offering the needed resources to a garden or backyard habitat, you are spreading a blessing. And it is easy to spread blessings in the world in many other ways, for example, by sending out a prayer or an intention toward something or someone. Follow the slogan that was popular in America a few years ago: "Practice random acts of kindness and senseless acts of beauty." We can be the perpetrators of drive-by blessings and random magical acts of healing. (It's a good bet these acts won't make the headlines, but how infinitely preferable such random acts are than those regularly given prominence in the headlines and nightly news.) I have often sent healing energy to strangers on buses or trains or subways, in the supermarket, on the street, or wherever I encounter them. If someone looks sad or is struggling visibly with some emotion or condition, we can send them healing energy on the spot. Quietly, eyes open, with practice you can mentally project the colors we discussed in chapter 1: pink light for love, and blue light for healing, white for protection. You can project those energies at anyone or anything, unbeknownst to them. This is not so very different from smiling at someone and sending them a happy thought—just a bit more focused and purposeful. These are simple magical acts available to everyone. True "practical magic"!

We have begun practicing the ability to project energy, which is one of the fundamental concepts of magic. Now we will combine the exercise above, where we offered water as part of balancing a habitat, with a next step, the magical ability to endow that water with special energy.

Exercise 7: Blessing Our World with Water

In this exercise we will project a blessing or healing energy into the water in the garden or habitat we created in exercise 6. In Wicca this technique is called "charging," filling the water, or some object, with the desired energy. It thus becomes an additional gift to our environment.

Touching the water that will grace your green space, or that you will use to water your plants, center yourself and connect with your deeper, internal, quiet self. Connect with the feeling you had when you were in Nature in exercise 4, the first exercise in Sense Awareness.

The element of water has many gifts, both on the physical level and the metaphysical. It offers us the gift of life, of growth, and of cleansing—our planet as we know it could not exist without water. Traditionally in metaphysical work, the element of water also represents the spiritual gifts of love and compassion.

Using the element of water and its many gifts, see that physical water in your hands glowing a beautiful sparkling blue. Visualize how it sparkles and radiates with magical, healing energy. See in your mind's eye how that energy will infuse the earth where you pour it, or how it will heal and bless the land where you leave it. Perhaps the animals who drink it will gain health and happiness and safety from the water you now charge with gifts and magical energy.

When you have visualized that transferal of energy from you to the water, gently let the image go. It is completed. You do not need to think about it anymore. Bring your awareness back to the room or the open space where you stand. Then continue with your day or evening.

You are truly embarked on your journey as a Deep Ecologist and an Earth Magician.

Charging water is a magical act. It is easy to overlook such simple acts, but these very acts bring us more and more in tune with Gaia. First we learned to connect with the energies around us, using our bodies and minds as means of channeling these energies for our own and others' protection. Now we have practiced projecting these same energies. It is easy to overlook the simplest acts that lead us to becoming more in tune with Gaia. We must always remember how even small steps lead us closer to the divine in Nature and to the deep interconnectedness that is magical Deep Ecology.

Gaia Goals

☀ Always remember the web of life and the need for balance.

☀ Make a haven for wildlife and all forms of Nature in your backyard, on your deck, in your local park, in your place of work or school.

For more details, the National Wildlife Federation has instructional starter packets to help you create a Backyard Wildlife Habitat.

Visit www.nwf.org/habitats or call 1-703-438-6100, in the United States.

☀ Never use pesticides or harmful chemicals in your home, yard, garden, or driveway.

☀ Cherish the precious elixir water. Never waste it, and find creative ways to conserve it, for example, flush toilets less often, save used but clean water for watering plants, share showers, and so on—use your imagination.

☀ Consider your purchases for the next two weeks in light of our discussion of sacrifice and balance. Ask yourself: "Am I buying this as 'retail therapy' or is this something I really need? Does it have too much packaging? Could I find something simpler and less-environmentally destructive that would work as well?"

☀ As you decide what you can release from your life on the material plane—personal belongings, sports equipment, office equipment — charge these things with blessings for the next users. Use the technique you have learned to spread blessings!

Chapter 3
Nature's Feedback Loop to Healing

... every tree, every stone, every breath of air, every rat's tail—
all that is yourself;
there is nothing that is not yourself.

Carl Jung

Some Deep Ecologists never get out into Nature. Many don't have the time, luxury, or access to the wilderness. Others even claim that the best way to live lightly on the planet is to leave Nature alone. There are people, environmentalists of certain philosophies, who believe that the best place to live if one is truly concerned about the environment is in the city, in a small apartment. I appreciate the concept of leaving the wilderness to wild things and the cities to people. However, I think that as Earth Magicians and activists we absolutely need to have some Nature contact from time to time. It not only has far-reaching beneficial effects on our health, but it also strengthens the connection that calls us to heal Gaia. Contact with Nature renews our magical health and vitality, as it rests our minds and charges our bodies. My philosophy and that of the Gaia Group (GG)/Temple of Gaia way of Wicca sees Nature as the great teacher and healer. I believe we begin to be healed as soon as we step in to Nature wholly *conscious,* awake to the contact we are making.

As the more primal magical beings they are, children can easily make this connection. We adults may lose the ability from living "in our heads," as the expression goes—living cerebrally or intellectually controlled lives. Our jobs, our worries, the frenetic pace of modern life all break that natural bond. The environments we create for ourselves also influence how we feel "in ourselves," how easily we can relate to Nature and natural beings. Fluorescent lighting, computers, microwave ovens, cellular phones all sap our vitality, that current of energy running through us that Asian philosophy calls chi or ki (pronounced "chee" or "key"). Time with Nature cleanses and strengthens our chi while getting us "out of our heads," helping to still the chatter in our brains. This, in part, causes the joyous, sensual rush of energy we may experience from having contact with Nature or performing sacred ritual. Our chi flows more powerfully and connects us with the vital force of Nature.

My family and I feel very fortunate that we live in the Rocky Mountains and can make this direct connection on a regular basis. However, it is possible, even while living in suburban or urban settings, to find places where Mother Earth's vital signs and pulse can be felt. I know this intimately, for I grew up in the Hudson Valley of New York State, just twenty miles from Manhattan; I have also lived in London, as well as other large cities. In each of these I have sought and found beautiful, soul-renewing groves, brooks, lakes, woodlands, meadows, beaches, or riverbanks where I could encounter the old Gods and Goddesses, as well as the Elemental folk, the Nature spirits.

Pagans and Wiccans frequently seek out these urban pockets of Nature. I have witnessed stirring rituals created in city parks that help to satisfy the soul hunger of the participants, while restoring and nourishing their relationships with the Gods. In these urban or suburban settings, the Elementals and the Gods may need a little coaxing at first to come forth from their "caverns deep"—but come they will! Once met and honored in the Magic Circle, they will be waiting the next time you stop the mundane world to create sacred space. In Wicca we call the Magic Circle the "World between the Worlds," and never does that phrase fit so well as when the Circle is cast with skyscrapers or townhouses in the not-too-distant periphery. Then we truly have created a place of retreat and of sanctuary between the modern world and the realm of the Gods.

For those new to the occult arts, "Casting the Circle," a term used in magic and in Wicca, means the act of creating, through action, visualization, and will, a sphere-shaped sacred space that protects all within by a magical barrier. The space is also appropriately cleansed and blessed to welcome the Gods. The Temple of Gaia style of Wiccan Circle Casting is given in appendix B.

In this chapter, we'll focus on consciously reconnecting with the natural world. Separation from the world is an illusion, as is the sense of separation from our fellow humans. As you work the exercises here, strive to lose your feeling of separateness from Nature. You'll use talismans and the technique of pathworking to bring yourself into the wild, and you'll find your Root place, that place (or object) that best grounds you in your spiritual power. Finally, you'll cultivate a deeper compassion for Earth and all her children. All these techniques, including the work on an enhanced sense of compassion, tie back into our magical toolkit.

Pathworking as a Tool for Reconnecting with Nature

Whether by choice or necessity, we may not have physical contact with Nature as often as our spirits need it. How wonderful, then, that practitioners of magic have the ability to psychically transport themselves to a place in Nature. Through a regular practice of visualization, meditation, and the guided visualizations called pathworkings, it is possible to be in whatever setting you choose at any time.

After you do the Deep Relaxation and the Connection and Protection exercises you learned in previous chapters, I will guide you through two pathworking exercises in which you'll transform into a being from the wild, then experience living in the wild as that being. You can use these techniques whenever you feel the need to connect more deeply with Nature but can't *physically* make that connection.

You've already learned a few basic pathworking skills. In this next exercise, you will journey deeper.

Exercise 8: Becoming Wild, Becoming Ancient

Sit or lie down in a very quiet place, where you will not be disturbed for a while. Turn off your phone if you are at home or have a cell phone. Begin with the relaxation exercise you learned in exercise 1. Then connect and protect yourself with the techniques you learned in exercise 2. Now you're ready to be transported to the wild.

In your mind's eye see yourself transforming into different beings. Don't simply observe. Feel yourself becoming other people, other beings.

Some possibilities:

🔅 Become an indigenous person of the past.

Feel how an ancient forest dweller or a sea coast native or a native of the desert would sense the natural world. Ask yourself: "What kind of structure do I live in? What do I wear? What kind of hair do I have? How does the ground feel under my feet? Are my feet bare? If not, what kind of foot covering am I wearing? What foods do I eat?" Try to answer these questions as the indigenous person.

🔅 Become an animal or a bird.

Find out what kind of covering you have: fur, scales, feathers, skin? How long are your legs? Or do you have fins, or flippers? What does it feel like to fly, or slither, or run like the wind?

> When do you sleep? What do you eat? What sound do you
> make to call a mate or when you are frightened?

Whatever you have chosen to experience, *truly* become it. Live its every
mood; through it, sense every minute change in the environment.
Breathe as it. Feel it in your every muscle, every pore; know it in your gut.

Experience this deep sense of transformation for as long as you
can—twenty minutes, half an hour, an hour?—before returning from
deep relaxation. Repeat this exercise whenever you can.

Exercise 9: Deeper Wild and Ancient Senses

Keeping the new awareness you experienced in exercise 8, return to deep
relaxation and again connect and protect.

Walk through the environment you've chosen. Take in every little
detail. Again think how the being you have become would sense things;
let yourself *experience everything* as that being.

When you are ready, go deeper. Sense how a tree would experience
the world, a rock, a mountain, a wave, the air, a cloud. Live with that
knowledge and that empathy for a little while. Becoming an animal of
another species is one thing. Becoming something of an entirely different makeup, of a totally different molecular structure is something else.

See what messages those other parts of Nature have for you. What
deeper knowing do you receive from sensing, breathing, or being still as
they are?

When you are ready and you feel you have taken as much experience as you need for now, come back from deep relaxation.

Doing these exercises as often as possible will help you develop the
bond and awareness with Nature you need as a foundation to your
Nature Magic and Deep Ecology. The honor and the risk you take on
yourself is ever deepening your oneness with Mother Gaia. This deepening bond will enhance your magical power as it heals and strengthens your chi, your magical vitality. Magic is already at work in you and
through you! As you further connect with the energy of the planet and
her many beings, you are truly beginning to sharpen your psychic senses.

Exercise 10: More Wild Senses—Sensing Energy Fields

The energy field, or aura,[4] is the extension beyond the body of any being's personal vital force. It can extend as little as a few centimeters or as much as a meter or more. The color changes depending on the condition of the person or entity—this field is directly connected with the health and status of the being. It may first be perceived as just a shimmer in the air.

This exercise will help beginning practitioners to start seeing auras—particularly auras in Nature. I remember the first time I saw my own aura in its full beauty. I was doing yoga and watching myself in a mirror. I suddenly saw what appeared to be an "aurora borealis" hovering around my head and shoulders. I was completely taken aback at first and thought, "What are those lights?" Then to my delight I realized that I was seeing my aura. By developing this awareness, one can see trees breathe, sense their feelings, hear their voices and the other voices of Nature, such as those of the Elementals.

Here we will initiate this clairvoyant ability and work toward a healing practice using auric energies. Clairvoyance *is a traditional term used to describe the psychic ability to see energy or spirits. (*Clairaudience *is the ability to hear sounds or voices others do not hear, such as those of Angels or Elementals, trees, animals, and others.)*

Begin with the relaxation technique. When you are truly relaxed, open your eyes.

Maintain your deeper state of consciousness while looking around you. This is a very important skill in itself for magic and ritual. It is a kind of split or "blended" consciousness. Study the tree branches or leaves above you. See the light that seems to emanate from them. This is their aura! At first you may only see a shimmer in the air around the branch or leaf or trunk. However, as you practice, you will begin to see actual colors and a larger field of energy.

Focus on the grass's aura. Continue with all of the natural beings around you. Is there a dog or cat or bird nearby? Study them too. These vital beings often have a more easily notable energy field than a human being.

Now look at your own hands—or at yourself in the mirror. Keep focused and in a deeply contemplative or light trance state. You will begin to see your own energy field!

Slowly, begin to tune back in to the more "mundane" side of life and draw your awareness back in to the modern world. Eat or drink something to ground yourself once more.

Magical Activism through Pathworking

In this next pathworking, you will learn to lay down deeply magical earthward roots by choosing a "Root," an object or place that will become (or is already) a personal power center and a sacred site or object for you. This exercise is adapted from my tradition's Book of Shadows.

We have talked about being in and honoring Nature, wherever we may choose and however we may access it. Now you will define a place that is sacred to you personally, a place that heals you as you heal and protect it. You will begin to connect to the awesome loop that is part of Earth healing.

Exercise 11: Connecting with Your Root

Choose a place in Nature that you are particularly drawn to, a place that you have felt yourself "resonate" to. Choose a place that is special to you beyond all others, where you feel safe and whole and at home. This is your "Root."

Your Root might be a place where you go from time to time to reground and center yourself. Or it may be a place from the past that you now visit only in your mind. An object that brings your spirit the same kind of "connectedness" and serenity may function as your Root . . . perhaps a crystal, a rock, or something from your favorite spot. Choose what works best for you. The point is that you feel deeply connected to your chosen spot in Nature or your object.

Trees, stones, wells, streams, lakes, grottoes, groves, beaches, shorelines, riverbanks, mountain meadows, woodlands, or peaks—any natural place that touches your heart's core—can function as your Root. You will feel serene and strong when you find your place. Maybe it will feel "like home."

Now that you have chosen your Root, stand before it or in it (if it is a place in Nature), hold it, or visualize doing so. Address it now as a friend; greet your Root place or object with love and compassion. Gently touch it and feel its harmony and rhythm, and know that, in its own way, it is touching you also.

Begin to feel currents of energy flow between you and your Root. Gradually feel both yourself and the object glowing a rich blue that slowly deepens to an intense indigo. Let compassion and empathy flow between you and your Root.

When you are feeling both yourself and the object glowing a dark indigo, ask permission to step into the Root. If you feel it is granted, then do so. You have now merged with another state of being, with another kind of consciousness. Relax into it. Allow yourself to sit in that awareness and be the other. Be at one with it for as long as you wish. Attempt to find out its true name; feel as it does; feel that you are eternal, as it is. Ask whether you may serve it and how you may serve it; discover what it needs. See if there is some way that it may serve you in return. If words do not come, let images or sensations run through you and wash over you. Remember: words are a human construction. Emotions and images are ways of communicating too.

You are ancient as your Root is . . . let yourself connect through your Root with that sense of age once more. It will help to lead you to the sources of ancient wisdom and knowing in yourself.

When you have finished communing and communicating, thank the object or the place, and bid it farewell for now. Gradually and gently depart from it.

Remember: your Root is an ally and an aid to you. It will support you and assist you in many ways; in times of trial and upset, you can draw power and sustenance from your Root. Therefore, honor this special site by offering libations of food or wine, tobacco or cornmeal. You may also offer services to the place, such as those suggested below. If your Root is a place on the earth plane, you can honor it in the physical sense. If not, you can make those offerings on the astral plane, in a psychic sense. Or you may simply transmit white light to surround it, as an offering of protective, healing energy. It is good to work magic at a Root site of your own, to try to connect with the Spirit of that place through ceremony. If it feels sacred to you, it may well have an ancient history of being used for ceremonies and, therefore, will have a particularly strong Spirit connected with the land.

The sense of Root has many meanings. In the next chapter we will begin to explore the system of opening the chakras to work with your body's energies. You have a chakra often called "root" at your sexual center, in your groin area. I discussed earlier the sensual and often erotic connection that being in Nature can evoke at times as well as the sensuality of Earth religions. If merging with your Root place brings up sensual or erotic feelings for you, explore why that is and, most of all, how that can be healing for you. It comes from your wild self, your true and ancient self, which has never been wounded by repressive social conventions and mores. Let those energies flow. They are healing in themselves and are part of the Gaian loop we have talked about. Consider it a gift from Mother Gaia.

In terms of the service you may offer to your Root in return, if you have chosen an actual physical place in Nature, you can go there with the practical intent of acting as its guardian. For example, check it from time to time to be sure no one has damaged it by their use or to clean up any garbage that you find. If you have chosen a wilderness area or a park, and there is any danger of it being developed, start a campaign to protect this place. Write letters to your representatives, start a petition among those who also care about it, do whatever you can to ensure its protection as a wild place for the future. This is a way of living out your love for this place and of thanking it for the centering, healing energy it has transmitted to you.

Some may remember the slogan propagated by the fine organization Friends of the Earth: "Think globally, act locally." Make this a part of your life every day. In ministering to Gaia, our service begins on the smallest and most intimate levels.

Talismans

We adults tend to accumulate and use "stuff," material things, often forgetting the objects' symbolic or spiritual aspects. Material things store energy. Anyone who has kept a gift from a departed parent or grandparent, or from another significant person, knows full well what this can mean. A ring, a watch, a book, a pocketknife, or any thing from a beloved one now crossed over to the next life becomes a precious keepsake. I never knew my great-grandparents, nor did my husband know his. However, the pieces of furniture we have inherited from those ancestors mean a great deal to both of us as a connection with the past and with those whose lives made us who we are in so many ways.

Do clothes and other products made in sweatshops hold the energies of pain, anger, or sorrow? I am sure they do. Do you want that in your home or on your body? On your children's bodies? Think about that. If we all stopped and paid attention to the origins of our things, and to their symbolic significance, we would be less likely to fall prey to the "disposable society" attitudes. Such attention would cause us to buy things more mindfully, use them more mindfully, and not dispose of them so quickly and thoughtlessly.

The ability to discern the energy patterns, imagery, and messages emanating from certain objects can also be extremely useful in magical work. Witches and psychics can do this, as can children, who also intuitively sense the energy vibration or frequency residing in certain natural objects. Ever since my daughter was a toddler, she has collected rocks and shells from special places we have visited. At first we tried to discourage it, thinking it was just the whim of a young child. However, she has astonished us by knowing, even years later, where each one came from. Some children instinctively set up what amount to little altars with their favorite, special souvenirs and mementos. Children naturally resonate to the energy around and in these objects.

Among my many treasured objects from precious places, I have pieces of driftwood and shells from the Hudson River. I also have stones and other objects from special places in the U.K., Ireland, Italy, Chile, and other places. If I wanted to send healing energy to the Hudson or those other sites, I could use the objects I collected there as channels for that energy. This is an example of "talisman" magic. The object becomes a talisman that, in essence, can help you reach the place you wish to heal or send protection to. A talisman represents that place "in effigy," symbolically. In its very molecules live the vibration of its motherland, its origins. It is a living, tangible connection to the energy of that land and to the Spirits of that land. Like the Universe's imprint in our own souls and our own deepest molecular makeup, like the cosmic spiral of our DNA, we connect to our origins—"As the Universe, so the soul."

In their excellent book on spellcraft, *Spells and How They Work*, well-known Wiccan authors and scholars Stewart and Janet Farrar dedicate a chapter to talismanic magic. I often use the following quotation from there in my classes: "A talisman is, so to speak, the concentration of the meaning and intent of a spell into a pocketable or wearable form. It is a personal thing, for the protection, encouragement, strengthening or what-have-you of the individual who carries or wears it. It is much more tailor-made than a mere amulet, which is generalized, such as the traditional rabbit's foot or St. Christopher medal."

You can work with the energy vibration of your Root object, or another special object or talisman, in order to send healing and protection to a place dear to you. You can perform this act of healing and protection whenever and as often as you like.

Exercise 12: Meeting Your Root Talisman

First, choose a special object and set it apart from all others. You may want to honor it by keeping it on your personal altar, if you have one, or in some other special place.

As you embrace deep relaxation, make direct contact with your talisman. Hold it in your hand or lay it on your body if you are lying down. Place it on your forehead, between your eyebrows in the region of your "Third Eye," the center of your psychic vision or over your heart, center of compassion.

Think of the place in Nature where that object originated. If it is a crystal, where might it have come from? The Rocky Mountains? The Appalachian Mountains? Africa? South America? Asia? The Middle East? An ocean beach you loved? If it is a rock you picked up somewhere, where did you find it? Try to identify the origin of your Root object, if you are not sure. Feel a sense of the energy of that originating place. Let energy flow between you and your talisman and allow yourself to see what images or messages come to mind.

You can also connect with the object's origin through what the object symbolizes to you. If it is a shell you love and resonate to, perhaps you can send healing to the ocean or a river through it—perhaps to the specific waters it came from. If it is a piece of wood, natural or carved, think of a forest you can send protection to. Maybe you know which forest the wood came from.

Visualize as you did when you sent colored frequencies of energy and light to Gaia in exercise 3 and to the water blessed in exercise 7. Envision an indigo light, the healing power of the Universe. See it wrapped around your Root talisman. It is glowing with that blue light, immersed in it and permeated with it.

Now envision the place that your talisman represents or comes from. For example, if it is a shell from the Pacific Ocean, see the beaches you know and love clean and vibrant. See the ocean teeming with fish, dolphins, whales, every kind of life. If it is a rock from a meadow, see that meadow peaceful and healthy. See wild animals—deer or elk or rabbits—grazing, playing, or dozing in the sun there. See rain falling and nourishing the plants there. Let your mind create the healthiest, most balanced environment for your Root talisman's home. And let the images that come of their own flow . . . but keep them centered and with the purpose of healing.

After you have seen life in balance and health there, envision the place you love glowing with the indigo that you are sending it.

If your Root place is an actual healthy wild place, just see it as it is, and surround it with white light in order to preserve and protect it.

If it feels right to you, call upon some form of the Deity to aid you in this magical work. Some examples from Wicca include Cernunnos, the Celtic Lord of the forests, animals, and wild places, and Demeter, Greek Goddess of grain and agricultural fertility. Some Wiccans call upon the Egyptian Goddess Isis (also honored throughout the Mediterranean) in her aspect as a Goddess of healing magic, or her mate, Osiris, who was connected with the fertility of the Nile. You might ask assistance from the indigenous tradition's deities you feel comfortable working with. Or, simply, "Dear God/Dear Goddess, please bless and protect this beautiful place" will do very nicely till you formulate a blessing in a way more personal to you.

Now slowly, gently bring your consciousness back from deep relaxation.

You have performed an act of healing and protective magic with your Root talisman. It is a common practice in magic to wrap any special object in cloth; for example, we do that with some of our ritual tools in Wicca. It is also a Wiccan technique to wrap a talisman after performing an act of magic with it. So it would be appropriate to now wrap your talisman in a piece of cloth; silk or natural fabric is usually deemed to be the best. And do not think or talk about the work you have done for a few days at least.

Before we proceed to other important magical concepts, I'd like to comment on attitudes about talismans and other honored objects. In ancient times, Pagans were criticized for "worshiping idols" because of the way they treated the statues of their Gods and Goddesses. It is a mistake to think that we worship the object itself. It is the energy or the Divinity represented by that object that we venerate. It would be easy to make that mistake, certainly, watching a worshiper kneeling at an altar or other place; however, it is important to make that distinction. Likewise the Druids and Celtic peoples were criticized for worshiping trees and wells and so on. However, they were honoring the Divine energy immanent in that place or that aspect of Nature, as indigenous people in North America and elsewhere did (and still do) with their sacred sites. We no more worship the actual thing than a Catholic worships a statue of the Virgin Mary or a Buddhist worships a statue of Buddha. Instead these people honor what the statues represent—Mary or Buddha. As apparent as that may seem to some, it bears discussion for those largely unfamiliar with Paganism and Wicca.

Widening Your Circle of Compassion

The exercises so far in this chapter have focused on creating and cementing your reconnection with Nature and your Root place; you have begun to meld your consciousness with the many aspects of Gaia and divinity all around you. The following quote, attributed to the great scientific genius Albert Einstein, aptly expresses the importance of growing beyond the sense of separateness:

> A human being is a part of the whole, called by us "Universe," a part limited in time and space. She/He experiences herself/himself, her/his thoughts as something separated from the rest . . . a kind of optical delusion of her/his consciousness.

> This delusion is a kind of prison for us, restricting us to our personal desires and to affection for a few persons nearest to us.

> Our task must be to free ourselves from this prison by widening our circle of compassion to embrace all living creatures and the whole of nature in its beauty.

So many things in our lives are illusion, or *maya* as the Hindus term it. These exercises will help to widen your circle of compassion, a beautiful phrase. You will find it progressively less easy to step on an insect thoughtlessly, or to cut down a tree needlessly, after you consistently practice these exercises for a time. I have gone to the extreme at times: I even carry Black Widow spiders out of the house. I do not want them near my children, but I recognize they have a place in the great scheme of things and a right to live. They, like so many creatures we humans may find loathsome, are part of Gaia, too.

So many of our family on this planet, human and nonhuman, are in need and in pain. We each have our unique interests, skills, and abilities that we can call upon to help our compassion grow. The best path is to find some kind of altruistic activist work or consciousness raising that our souls resonate to. Such a response, in whatever work we choose, will help us to commit our time and talents. As we offer our efforts in service, we evolve as a species, and the consciousness evolving across our world grows. Here are a couple of examples of finding compassionate work that suits the individual. Some years ago, I was working for a wildlife campaigning organization in the U.K. as a dolphin and whale campaigner. At the same time, my sister was working with handicapped children in the United States. She became a foster mother, taking into her home the most devastatingly ill and disabled babies and children. I was reading and writing about dolphins' or whales' deaths, but she was holding the babies when they died.

Obviously I admire inexpressibly the work she and other people do in the healing professions. Nevertheless, I do not belittle my own efforts or the amazing work of other animal activists and environmentalists. My sister has a gift with sick children that I do not have. Many of my gifts and passions are different from hers. (Of course I frequently send magical energy to her and to her children, as well as pray for them.) All kinds of activist, caring work helps to develop our compassion, our power, and our connection to Gaia.

We are all, every being, interconnected through a complex circuitry of energy. Our ancestors knew and recognized this, and now modern science is giving names to it. Studies such as Quantum Physics, Chaos Theory, String Theory, and so on recognize dimensions of existence and energy networks previously sensed by only the most intuitive or most highly trained. This concept of interconnectedness is key in magic.

As you develop your unique forms of magical activism, you might consider the Karmic Law of Threes, sometimes also called the Karmic Law of Retribution. In essence, this law teaches that all of our actions come back to us threefold. This law of magical working keeps us tuned to the highest and most ethical purposes, even if partially through a desire for self-preservation! If all of our actions will return to us thrice over, then obviously we want to behave in the most conscientious and scrupulous manner, in magic and in life.

However, this teaching has another element to it that helps to explain the miraculous feedback loop we experience through healing magic and the projection of altruistic energies. Since everything we do comes back to us threefold, so does the healing that we send out to the planet and to all other life-forms. Therefore, one great occult mystery and secret is revealed: as you heal, so shall you be healed. An incredible, cosmic "tit for tat" with superb results! We do not go into the healing arts for that self-serving goal, but it is a wonderful "bonus" that we receive for our good works.

Persevere in your work on the twelve exercises given thus far. Remember that magic is flowing through you and throughout your life. You are a channel for healing. These exercises and practices are essential to your growth as Earth Stewards and Earth Healers. Gaia will thank you.

🔅🔅🔅🔅🔅🔅🔅

Gaia Goals

Protect our wild places in every way that you can.

🔅 Stay informed about current legislation affecting the wilderness. Write letters and make phone calls to your representatives and government officials to voice your opinions. Let them know you believe in preserving the wilderness. Letters can hugely influence policy making.

🔅 Remember the old sayings "Take only photographs, leave only footprints" and "Pack it in, pack it out"? When in Nature, always walk, hike, climb, or camp responsibly and sustainably.

🔅 Never foul water sources with your campsite. Set your campsite at least 200 feet from any creek or river, any riparian area. Never leave toilet tissue on the ground; either bury your waste, or yes— pack it out! (Camping stores sell special bags for that.)

🔅 Remember that we share our habitat with wild animals, and we have taken over their homes. Be responsible toward their needs and habits. We can live safely with wildlife through thought, preparation, and conscientious living. When camping, leave no garbage or trace of your visit behind.

If you camp in bear country, hang your food, pans, packs, and so on in a tree at night.

🔅 It *is* all right to leave behind a blessing! While you're in the wild places, leave some of the magic energy you have learned to project. Offer a psychic gift to the Elementals, Guardian Spirits, and other beings who live there.

Chapter 4
Portals and Guides into the Elemental Kingdom

> The fairies have never a penny to spend,
> They haven't a thing put by,
> But theirs is the dower of bird and of flower
> And theirs is the earth and the sky.
> And though you should live in a palace of gold,
> Or sleep in a dried up ditch,
> You could never be poor as the fairies are,
> And never as rich.
>
> *Rose Fyleman*

The Elemental beings, Nature spirits, and rulers of the Nature Kingdoms can help us to enter and, if we are very lucky, to bond with that elusive, immortal, and nonhuman dimension of the earth around us. Like many Wiccan and Pagan practices, such communion is almost a kind of shamanic practice, allowing us to enter into another realm of consciousness and thereby work *within* it. By developing a relationship with the denizens of this mysterious dimension, we learn how to better communicate with Gaia, to help her on the deepest and clearest levels.

But who are these usually unseen helpers and allies? Before we talk about the magic we can make with them, let's examine who they are.

Devas, Faery Folk, Angels, and Other Guides

The Elemental Kingdom is the level of energy and vibration slightly less corporeal than our own, though it is still connected intrinsically to the earth plane. Within it live many beings, called by myriad names in the world's traditions and immortalized in legend the world over. In Wicca the Elemental beings are frequently known as gnomes and dwarves (earth), sylphs (air), salamanders (fire), and undines (water). Other traditions simply lump them together under the term *deva*. Deva is actually a Hindu term that refers to spirits, in a sense minor Gods, whose job is to care for Nature—an Eastern version of the Victorian "Flower Fairies." Buddhism also has a belief and a tradition of honoring the spirits connected with the different elements.

However, this is just the beginning. It has taken me years of practice to learn that these realms, other dimensions that exist—generally unseen—simultaneously with us here on Earth, are teeming with Nature spirits of many kinds. Some we simply do not have names for yet. In the European traditions, if you are of Irish descent, you will think of leprechauns and Faery Folk, the wee people and banshees. If you are Celtic from other lands, you will remember pixies and will-o'-the-wisps; or perhaps that spirit similar to the banshee that the Bretons call the ankhou. Every land and every language has its own names and characteristics for these magical beings. The ancient Greeks and Romans called them many things, some of which are echoed in the Wiccan nomenclature of sylphs, undines, and salamanders. Remember the dryads and naiads, tree and water spirits of Greek mythology? The nymphs and fauns cavorting in the spring sunshine with Pan as he pipes merrily? These are not simply legends, but true scenes, invisible to most.

When I cast a Circle, depending on where I am in the world and who the participants in the Circle are, there may well be Elementals I normally would not see, or may never have seen before. If someone visiting your Circle has a relationship with certain beings unfamiliar to you, you may have additional visitors you did not expect! For example, when I initiated a Priest who works closely with the dragon kingdom, although I had never had any experience of dragons, dragons suddenly appeared in the Circle when we called up the Watchtowers. (Seeing them was rather a shock initially, I must admit. They did not look like the Disney or Hollywood versions; I was not sure what kind of being I was seeing at first.) Likewise when I had a new member of the coven who had previously studied North American shamanism, there were frequently coyotes and bison in the quarters of the Circle. At first this too greatly surprised me. However, I quickly learned the connection and am very grateful for all the Elementals' willingness to participate in our human rituals. It has led me to learn about these varied powerful helpers, so that I now have a relationship with them and can work magic with them myself.

Many New Age spirituality practitioners casually throw out the term *Guides*. This can be very confusing to those who are new to the magical arts or who have ventured recently into alternative religion. Guides usually refers to "Spirit Guides," the astral-plane dwellers who help each person achieve his and her destiny in this incarnation. Some of these helpers are actually Angels, like the Christian guardian angels; some are human spirits between lives, or who will not incarnate again. Some, as is taught in Ceremonial Magic, are our own spirit's "Higher Self," that part of our soul that does not incarnate with us, but dwells in the highest levels of the spirit world—keeping watch, as it were. Many times the voices that people in danger or difficulty hear, voices that guide them or stop them from harm, are their own "Higher Self." At death we are reunited with that fragment of our souls to assess this life and to learn what lessons we should have taken on board here. Those who are very practiced in meditation, or in what shamanic practices call "journeying," (i.e., journeying or traveling to the spirit world in trance state), may be able to visit with these Guides at will to ask their advice and guidance. It is a marvelous technique and extremely helpful in our topsy-turvy world. We will explore a technique in chapter 5 to begin to build that ability.

For those who wonder where we fit in, humankind coexists on the earth plane with the Elemental rulers, the Lords and Ladies of the Watchtowers, and the Elemental beings (sylphs, salamanders, undines, gnomes, fairies, dryads, dragons, etc.). However, these beings are not quite as corporeal or of as heavy an energy vibration as most humans are. Maybe it is better to say that we are of slower vibration, and those beings of other planes are of a faster one. Beings that exist on higher planes, such as Angels or even Gods, can manifest themselves to humans who are able to see or hear them. We all know stories of such appearances. However, while not everyone is open or adept enough to see these manifestations of other realms of being, it is possible for everyone to have the ability. It simply takes time, concentration, faith, and dedicated practice. When we are of higher vibration it is easier to see and sense those beings that are not as corporeal as we are.

You are undoubtedly wondering what is required for this contact with the Nature Kingdom? In fact, the required abilities include many of the skills we have practiced in previous chapters:

- Deep relaxation
- Stilling the conscious mind
- Focus
- Visualization
- Belief

It also takes an open mind. (I can tell you that the Faerie Folk do not manifest themselves as we may expect!)

In addition to these talents, which can be practiced and developed, we should list psychic ability. Of course all humans have some psychic ability (as do all animals), although many people may not believe that they do. And everybody can, over time, develop that ability. However, some people's are more acutely noticeable at an early age. It is a true gift, although it often goes unappreciated. I was one of those psychically gifted children who probably make parents' lives . . . well, interesting. My childhood home in the magical Hudson Valley was a brick carriage house that had been built in the late nineteenth century. When I was very young I regularly woke my family up at night complaining about a man who came into my room or walked up and down the corridors. As a little child his nocturnal presence, unobtrusive though it was, bothered me. "Maybe it's the washing machine repairman who never showed up," my older sister said once in exasperation when I tried to wake her up, knowing that my parents had heard enough. Finally, teasing me about the man I frequently saw became a family joke. Consequently, over time I learned to live with the ghost who hovered around the house, and I learned not to talk about the fairies in the garden, or the voices of the trees and animals.

However, no matter how superb your psychic talents might be, you cannot become a Witch or Shaman or Healer overnight. The training required to become a true Healer, Shaman, or adept in magic takes many years—years of study, practice, and experience in which you learn to refine and use your natural powers. Not only does the training take time, but it is also the crucial evolution in your relationships with the Gods, with the Angels, and with the many dwellers in the Spirit Realms who are our helpers.

The techniques I offer here create a safe and thorough training regime in this process. In the first three chapters we made a good start with practices that not only aid in developing psychic abilities, but also aid in deepening our connections with Nature. Through these practices you can determine which techniques will help you most effectively in quieting your conscious mind's chatter and stilling the bustle of everyday life, while opening yourself to the magnificent, mysterious energy of the Universe. You have begun to learn how to still the mind and access deeper levels of your brain. This is the pursuit of all true seekers in any religion, and it is a quintessential aid in the ultimate goal of unifying with Spirit, with the All-That-Is.

The Root, Sensory Awareness, and other exercises began a process of training and conditioning the unconscious and conscious minds. As the old Jesuit adage advises: "Assume the position of prayer, and prayer will follow." Sometimes we may not feel ready to meditate, or to pray, or to do a ritual. Perhaps the day has been stressful, and it seems nearly impossible to shift that consciousness to a more spiritual, centered state. My life as a professional woman and a mom is often a hectic race from one activity to the next—from the office to the school to the soccer field. Therefore, I can vouch for the fact that it is essential to search out the personal triggers that signal our minds to slow down, to center, and to begin to shift brain state. Whatever the gesture, position, or action, it will work over time. On a more mundane level, it is similar to the effect of changing to work-out clothes, or putting on running shoes, hiking boots, or dance attire—suddenly you do feel like exercising, whereas you had no inclination moments earlier. The same thing happens in the theater: a miraculous transformation takes place when the actor first puts on a costume. The character he or she had been working to create suddenly becomes real and deeply integrated with the actor.

In some practices this shift in focus might come from chanting a certain sound or mantra, sitting in a certain position, lighting a candle. For a Catholic, Buddhist, Hindu, or Muslim perhaps it comes with picking up the rosary or prayer beads; for a Muslim, certainly the prayer rug itself aids in the mental shift. For Wiccans it might begin with lighting candles and incense, robing or disrobing, entering the Sacred Space, perhaps hearing certain music. In our tradition we perform a "Self Blessing," using consecrated water and oils to bless our bodies before the ritual begins. This begins the shift into the state of mind appropriate to ritual. The transition for Wiccans culminates in a total change of consciousness when the first words of the ritual begin—particularly when they are well-known and practiced passages, such as "The Witches' Rune." For others it may come with the first hymn the congregation sings, perhaps, or with the first prayers that are said by the rabbi, priest, or minister.

Let's look at another technique for centering, for relaxing deeply and opening to Divine influence through our own bodies' energy fields. This technique comes from Eastern teachings about the chakra system.

The Chakras

The concepts and techniques of working with the chakra system come originally from the ancient Hindu world. Using the chakra system is a time-honored method of meditation and of raising one's vibration. Hinduism is a living Pagan religion of enormous beauty, wisdom, and power that encompasses centuries of unbroken tradition. Many Wiccans practice various rites and meditations from it. Many also practice devotions to certain Hindu Gods and Goddesses. As I have said, Wicca is extremely eclectic and lends itself to an inclusive, international practice that draws from the pantheons of Gods and Goddesses of the world. So, while it is hard to pinpoint where the practice of working with the chakras came from in the Western Mystery Tradition, which Wicca is a part of, it is today of fairly widespread use outside of Asia.

There are seven primary chakras in the human energy field (see page 62). They are connected to seven principal glands in the body and help to circulate energy flows, thereby maintaining physical, emotional, and psychological health. They are seen to the psychic vision as a kind of lotus flower of wide petals, or sometimes simply as a disk. Healthy chakras spin in an orderly, clockwise direction. In fact, the word *chakra* means "wheel."

There is a significant dual sense of opening portals here. We open our own body's energy portals, the chakras, in preparation for finding portals into the Elemental Kingdoms. As you slow down, center, and open your chakras, you aid yourself in developing greater psychic sensitivity and awareness. It helps to connect you to your "authentic self," which can in turn help you to connect with the wilder, more ancient energies in Nature. The more you practice this, the more quickly you will be able to shift consciousness at will. To relate this directly to our work of healing Gaia, the chakras aid us in tuning in to Nature deeply and intimately enough to connect with the Elementals.

The next exercise offers a technique that I teach all my students and that I learned early in my studies of magic. I encourage students to practice it on a regular basis, until they are very adept at opening their chakras quickly and effectively. Before each Wiccan ritual begins, Initiates must silently perform a chakra opening in order to align themselves with each other and to prepare for entering Sacred Space.

Chakra work, like yoga (also of the Hindu tradition originally), Wicca, and other alternative spiritual practices, is involved with moving and directing energy. (There is one interpretation of the origin of the name Wicca that means to bend or shape. That is what we do with energy.) These techniques are also involved with healing through using energy. We are learning, in essence, to heal the earth and heal ourselves through an acutely sensitive awareness of energy. By opening your chakras regularly, as well as consistently practicing for weeks and months all the other exercises given here, you will feel a growing connection with the cosmic energies of the Universe. And, therefore, you will be ever more integrally connected with Gaia and with the primal forces of Nature. Finally, as part of this connection, you will be ready to meet the Elemental rulers, supreme allies in our work.

Exercise 13: Opening the Chakras

Like exercise 2, this practice will help you connect and protect. Begin with the relaxation technique from chapter 1.

Let your breath become deeper and even more relaxed. The belly muscles you may self-consciously hold in so often can loosen and relax, thereby letting more air into your body. Your belly drops down and you have a warm, rounded tummy, breathing more as a baby or an animal does. This is your center, the seat of your intuition and much of your healing power. Honor it as a center of power and let your muscles relax.

As you breathe in, once again envision a current of energy coming up from the earth to meet the base of your spine. At the base of your backbone, see a brilliant red disk, glowing and spinning, vibrant, alive. As we learned in exercise 2, this is your base chakra, which is where you connect to Earth energy. It should always be open and vibrant, keeping your vital energies healthy. Visualize that current of energy coming up to meet it and continuing through your body.

Now bring your awareness to your pelvic region. As you breathe in again, let that current of Earth energy come up past the spinning red disk to the next chakra, your root chakra at your sexual core. See a point of orange light there, which begins to slowly open. It gently unfurls itself like a flower bud; its petals open out and it too begins to spin.

As you breathe in, once more bring the current of energy up from the earth through your body—past the red disk, past the orange disk, and to your navel, your solar plexus. There see a point of yellow light begin to open, unfold itself, and spin like a beautiful yellow disk. Again, let your breath bring a current of energy up from the earth and through your body—up past the brightly glowing red, orange, and yellow disks, to your heart center, where a green point of light awaits. It too begins to open and unfurl itself. See it glowing a bright, healthy green and spinning gently.

As you breathe in once again, pull the Earth energy up through your body. See it flow up your spine, past the brightly whirling disks at

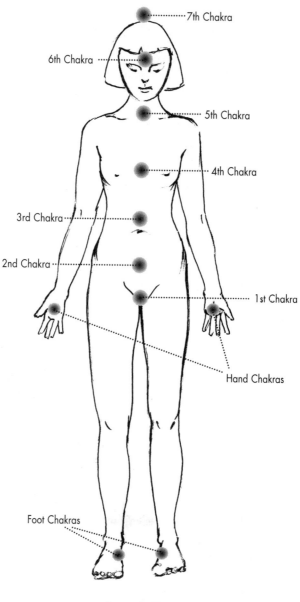

7th Chakra

6th Chakra

5th Chakra

4th Chakra

3rd Chakra

2nd Chakra

1st Chakra

Hand Chakras

Foot Chakras

The Chakras

your base, root, navel, and heart. It stops at your throat. There an aquamarine point of light begins to open out, to unfurl its petals, and to spin like the others.

Repeat the process, and as you bring the energy up your spine again, stop at the center of your forehead, where your "third eye" chakra is located. See it open out to a brilliant violet disk that slowly begins to whirl.

Again bring energy up through your body, past all the whirling disks along your center. Come to rest at the top of your head. There your crown chakra is already brilliantly glowing—like your base of spine chakra it must always remain open. It is an opalescent white, sparkling with energy. This is the part of your chakra system that connects you to Divine cosmic energy. Now as the Earth energy meets your crown chakra, see that sparkling white light spill over and cascade down you in a shower of white light. It reaches your feet and connects in a loop with the Earth energy there, rising through you again. Thus you are both filled and surrounded with Earth and Divine energy.

Remember: this is your birthright. You are a child of both the earth and the heavens. Remember that you can call on this energy at any time. You are protected by it—it forms a kind of protective shell or globe around you. Now you are ready to begin your deeper work.

Honor these centers of Divine wisdom and power in your body. As you learn to honor your body, you will treat it with more compassion and understanding. And as you treat your own body this way, so will you treat the earth's body with compassion and understanding. "As above, so below; / as the Universe, so the Soul; / as within, so without."

Bring your consciousness back to everyday reality, and ground yourself in it by eating or drinking to end this chakra session.

With this technique you are open and connected to the power of the Universe, but you are also protected. All deep meditations and all rituals, and in many cases divination, should begin with a connect and protect exercise like this one (or exercise 2). Truly I cannot reiterate the importance of this enough: *protection is essential for all magical work.* When the magical Circle is properly created and erected, it forms a completely safe, protected space for all the ritual participants to work within. However, when working alone without a complete Wiccan Circle, this kind of individual personal protection is a wise idea.

When you have finished with your meditation or journeying or ritual, you also should always close your second through sixth chakras. This will happen on its own when you eat or drink, or you can do it yourself in meditation by reversing the process described in exercise 13. Instead of visualizing the chakras opening as Earth energy rises to meet them, visualize the sparkling white energy of the crown chakra falling over each chakra and gently closing each in turn. Remember to leave the crown and base of the spine open. This is another way you can protect yourself from unwanted psychic influences, by bringing the five chakras—root, navel, heart, throat, and third eye—back to small points of light.

Finding the Doorways in Nature

> Open the door, the door which has no key,
> the door of dreams by which men come to Thee.

These evocative lines are from the "Invocation to the Horned God" and were written by the great occult author Dion Fortune. They are found frequently in the Wiccan Book of Shadows that many traditions draw inspiration from. The Horned God is an aspect of the Male Deity directly connected with Nature, with the woodlands and with animals—the Greek God Pan and other cultures' similar Nature Gods, such as the Anglo-Saxon Cernunnos or Herne. He is much honored and beloved in Wicca and modern Paganism, which is very likely the root of some confusion among Christian critics between Wicca and Satanism. Satan is a Christian belief; there is no Satan in Wicca or Paganism. (Although of course there is very definitely the concept of evil.) As Wiccans come "out of the broomcloset" so to speak, it will become easier to dispel some of these dangerous and divisive misconceptions.

As this invocation teaches, we must learn to find and open the doors to the Nature Kingdom in order to commune with the Elementals, as well as the Gods.

Marion Zimmer Bradley, the brilliant fantasy and science fiction writer who passed in 1999 into the Summerlands (as we call the afterlife in Wicca), described such gateways thus in *The Lady of Avalon:* "The Otherworld touches yours at many places, though there are not so many now as formerly. The stone circles are gateways, at certain times, as are all earth's edges—mountain tops, cavern, the shore where sea meets land."

What a beautiful idea: the earth's edges. The edges of the world, where two different natural phenomena meet, are notable. (Natural science recognizes that these meeting places of different ecosystems are unique. They are called "ecotones.") Edges, peripheries, wild far corners are where the Faery Folk are said to have been pushed—and then willingly stayed, off the human beaten tracks. We must go there to meet them—either physically or through meditation and pathworkings.

One of the best-known portals to the realm of Faery lies in the revered city of Glastonbury, England. Glastonbury is beloved by many of various denominations, Christian as well as Pagan, for its remarkable history and tangible enchantment. The famous Tor, a hill rising up in the middle of the city, has been a sacred site for centuries, about which many writers have speculated and rhapsodized. I made a "pilgrimage" of sorts there when revisiting England in 1997, taking precious time alone to reconnect with the Earth energies I had found there years earlier.

Revisiting Glastonbury Tor

Oh, Fisher King, who hides here the Grail;
Immortal Faery Lord obscuring the elfin trail!
Please let me run with your hosts once more,
On the spiral path to your realm's hidden door.

I shall bring you my searching mortal eyes
For you to teach where great knowledge lies.
The Earth Mother's arms reach out in embrace,
A bucolic landscape veils a sacred place.

But we who can see with vision's heart
May learn the Old Gods' magical art;
In great Avalon the veil is still thin
And we brave or foolish may dare venture in.

I have lived to travel many a long mile
With the Tor haunting me like a lost lover's smile.
Was it your realm of Faery I glimpsed long ago?
The spiral path to your Portal you deigned then to show.

I honor the Old Gods, the Sun, Wood, and Hill;
My life's in their service, my heart and my will.
I beg of you now—let me glimpse you again!
Faery Lord, Rex Arturus, Herne, Bride, Morgaine!

Show me not merely glamour, but deep knowledge and true.
Whether Avalon or the Rockies—I'll be waiting for you . . .

It is intriguing to note that many of these portals lie outside the "beaten path." Historically these outskirts of civilization are also where the Romans and invading tribes pushed the Celtic peoples—to the fringes of the British Isles and of Europe. In the United States, our government relegated the Native Americans to the fringes, edges, and outskirts. Native American reservations are frequently located in lands no one wanted: deserts, badlands, swamps. Such lands usually were not the places these Earth-honoring tribal cultures wanted, loved, or called home. However, in a strange and ironic twist, the wild edges of society can perhaps offer people who understand the Spirit realms and the Nature Kingdoms continued places of contact with the Otherworld on our increasingly urbanized planet.

Exercise 14: Finding a Personal Portal

Have you ever found a natural place that you hated to leave? Where you just wanted to stay forever? Did it actually affect your body when you stepped onto the earth there? Did you suddenly feel relaxed and happy? Comforted somehow? Even sleepy? Did you sit or lie down and feel transported in your mind or heart? Maybe it was the beauty of the place that resonated, the quiet, or simply the feelings the place gave you.

If you are very attuned to your psychic abilities, you may have noticed a heightened Earth energy at this place, a "vibration" or a strong sense of Gaia's pulse there. Perhaps the air actually shimmered with this energy. The trees and plants, grasses, water, stones, or sand, may have had a kind of "light" around them. If this sort of heightened sensitivity is familiar to you, you may have sensed other presences there in this vital, natural place. Did you ever turn suddenly, thinking you had seen something out of the corner of your eye, a presence or a flash of light, only to realize there was "nothing" there?

I have found these Portal places on riverbanks, beside creeks and brooks, on the ocean beach, in woodlands, in the mountains, and in lush, flower-filled gardens. These meeting places of our world and the Faery Realms can occur anywhere that Nature is vital and alive. You may find one in your own backyard as well as in the wilderness. You will know it by the sense you have in your body, in your mind, and in your spirit. You will always feel a "call," a pull; you will most likely want to sit down and stay awhile. And you will find yourself drawn back again and again.

Stop reading for a moment, close your eyes, and let your mind drift to one of these Portal places, some place in Nature that felt Otherworldly to you, a physical place on Mother Gaia's body that pulled at your heart and called to you. This may be the Root place we explored in exercise 11, or you may need to think back into your childhood, or to a vacation time.

Roam now in your mind at this Portal place. Enjoy visiting it again. Remember to honor this place and to thank both Gaia and the Elemental beings who live there. Like your Root, this is a place of sustenance and of spiritual growth for you, a place where you can touch Gaia and the Otherworld more readily.

In your own time, come back from this Portal place. Ground yourself in the way that works best for you.

Blessing Yourself as a Preparation and a Tool

One of the triggers or signals that helps members of the Temple of Gaia and the Gaia Group (GG) to shift consciousness before ritual or important magical work is the "Self Blessing." For those who already work in the magical arts, it will be familiar, as it uses much the same wording as the Wiccan "Fivefold Kiss." Used in rituals, the Fivefold Kiss is exchanged between Initiated Priests and Priestesses, or between magical partners. We honor the physical world in Wicca and Paganism as the place where Divinity is immanent, and we honor our bodies similarly.

Our bodies can become holy vessels for Divinity in ritual, where the Goddess or God is "drawn down," called to indwell the body of the properly prepared Priest or Priestess. This supremely magical act is without a doubt one of the most powerful that the occult arts offers Initiates. In the traditions of Wicca I've grown from, this act of essentially channeling or embodying such Divine energy in ritual is reserved only for Initiates. In fact, in GG practice, it is reserved only for High Priests and High Priestesses. In the Temple of Gaia, from First Degree, "properly prepared" Priests and Priestesses may begin to experience this extremely privileged rite. However, this differs widely from tradition to tradition in Wicca and Paganism.

This beautiful practice is one way that Wiccans and Pagans can "raise their vibration" and heighten the process of their spiritual evolution. However, all people, through spiritual work such as enlightened activism and altruistic work, through prayer and meditation, and through mindful living, can "raise their vibration." This is an expression found today in the occult arts and New Age philosophies that has very ancient roots. In some ways the idea of raising one's vibration is similar to the aim in following Buddhism's Eightfold Path, which advocates right views, right resolve, right speech, right conduct, right livelihood, right effort, right mindfulness, and right concentration.

Raising our vibration means becoming more spiritually evolved and closer to the Gods or God—more enlightened essentially—while still in the flesh. It refers back to the transcendental image of Divinity as "above" us; we need to bring our earthly bodies' energy vibration "up" to higher levels, although in the Pagan and Earth religion view, as well as others, those levels can be right here on Earth. Whatever the terminology, all true seekers pursue such evolution of the spirit through the religion or spiritual tradition they choose. This pursuit has been called "the Great Work" from time immemorial by metaphysical and occult thinkers. Indeed it is the greatest work, perhaps requiring various lifetimes.

Although the body is perceived as good and holy in Wicca, before ritual it is still appropriate to prepare it with a blessing. This practice may help some to center themselves and become more connected to the spiritual levels before any magical working, no matter how formal or simple. If two people are working together, it is a lovely way of honoring the Goddess within the woman or the God within the man.

A very simple act of consecration is needed before beginning the rite. You will need a bowl of salt and water, perhaps with a few fragrant herbs, flower petals, and oils in it. If you have performed a consecration before, then you can first consecrate the salt and water. If not, you may want to stand before the salt and water, focusing your mind on it, and speak a few words of blessing to it, in the names of whomever you see as Divine. Salt and water mixed together are frequently used in Wicca and Paganism for purification and protection.

Remember that like the energy we saw coming from the earth and the cosmos in exercises 2 and 13, you are a channel for powerful energies. This is the power you channel, or will, into the salt and water in a consecration. It is much the same as creating charged water, which you did in exercise 7. As you saw Gaia surrounded with healing blue energy in exercise 3, now see the water in the bowl permeated and filled with that kind of sparkling, magical blue light. You might like to hold your hand over it, or even put your right index finger into the water. You are channeling the magical blue energy through your body and your hand and into the water when you do that, a technique used very often in magic.

If you are an experienced Witch or Magician, and you have an "Athame," you may like to use it to charge the water. For those new to these paths, the Athame is one of the primary magical tools, traditionally a black-handled ceremonial knife or dagger, only used for ritual and magic. The Athame is not intended to be used for cutting and must never draw blood. If it does, it loses all magical potency. It is a symbol of air in most Wiccan traditions.

In exercise 17 we will meet the Elemental rulers. Let us prepare by practicing a self-blessing. This one is based largely on the form used by the Gaia Group and the Temple of Gaia. I suggest that you follow this form until you become comfortable with it, then feel free to create your own self-blessings. As our GG training paper, written to guide students, says: "As time goes on, you may develop your own form of the rite. This is fine as long as it has the desired results within yourself."

Exercise 15: The Self-Blessing

Prepare yourself with a relaxation exercise and perhaps a chakra opening. The self-blessing is particularly important if you are about to enter a full ritual, perform an important act of magic, or take part in any other significant act. It is also a very soothing and healing form of meditation that offers great healing effects. You might just like to end a stressful day with it, or use it to begin the day centered and cleansed spiritually. Remember: "As above, so below"—we honor our bodies, we balance our energies. In doing so, we can also honor Gaia and the many denizens of her various kingdoms. As our own bodies and energies are in balance, so can we balance the energies around us. Stand with your arms crossed across your chest with fingertips touching your shoulders, what occultists call the "Osiris position." When you are ready to begin, touch the water with your right hand. (If you choose, you may use consecrated oil in place of salt and water for this blessing.)

Touch the tops of your feet and say:
"Blessed be my feet that have brought me in these ways."

Touch the right hand to the water and then to both knees and say:
"Blessed be my knees that shall kneel at the sacred altar."

Touch the right hand to the water and then to the womb or genital area and say:
"Blessed be my sex without which we would not be."

Touch the right hand to the water and then to each breast and say:
"Blessed be my breasts erected in beauty and strength."

Touch the right hand to the water and then to the lips and say:
"Blessed be my lips that shall utter the sacred names."

Stand and commune with the Gods/Spirit/All-That-Is. Feel that you are centered, cleansed, purified. Feel a sense of harmony in your inner self. When you are ready, move on to the activity you have prepared for, or return to your reading.

Connecting with the Elements

In Paganism and Wicca, as well as other Earth-honoring paths, our bodies are not only seen as sacred, but they are also connected intrinsically to the sacred body of the earth. As James Lovelock wrote in the Gaia Hypothesis, we have a complex yet intimate connection with Gaia. Likewise we are connected to each of the elements not only physically, within our bodies, but also in our temperament and psychology.

Whether we live in an intensely urban environment or on the edge of the wilderness, because of our own unique makeup and personalities, one element can begin to dominate as we change and grow throughout our lives. By understanding which elements we are lacking in, and which we have an abundance, or perhaps an overabundance of, we can help to bring ourselves into balance. Astrology is one way of doing this. Astrology is an art, a therapeutic modality, and a science that can show in specific detail which elements most influence a person. By looking at the position of the planets at a person's birth, as well as at specific times throughout their lives, astrological studies can show which planets and which elements most influence a person.

Other techniques, like the one that follows, can also be used to focus on the elements and create a balance in our own temperaments, personalities, and emotions. Such elemental harmony will contribute a positive impact on your health and sense of well-being, and this, in turn, will have a positive impact on the service you can offer to Gaia and your fellow beings.

Let's begin by looking at the qualities and weaknesses attributed to each element by some of the most ancient sources—astrology, alchemy, Kabbalah, herbalism, even early medicine. Modern Asian medicine, such as Chinese herbalism and Indian Ayurvedic healing still practice this concept of restoring or strengthening health by bringing the elements into balance.

Air
Positive: keenness of mind, clarity of intellect, cerebral, intuitive in a rational sense, communicative

Negative: too heady, thought-bound, "spacey" (lacking in practicality, indecisive, cut off from emotions)

Fire
Positive: passionate, forceful, courageous, daring

Negative: impulsive, angry, overly passionate, not rational, "hot-headed"

Water
Positive: loving, compassionate, intuitive in a right brain/feeling sense, emotionally tuned in to others

Negative: wishy-washy, impractical, weak-willed

Earth
Positive: strong, persevering, dedicated, sensuous, practical, solid, dependable

Negative: stubborn, stolid, inflexible, unimaginative, vulgar

The following exercise can help to harmonize the influence of each element.

Exercise 16: Balancing the Elements in Ourselves

Prepare for this visualization by setting up representative examples of each element near where you will work. For example, as we discussed in exercise 6, you may choose incense to represent air, a candle or lamp for fire, a bowl of water for water. If you are outside, you can lay your hand on the earth; otherwise use a bowl of dirt as a representative.

Choose a quiet place for this exercise, preferably in Nature. It could be your Root place or your Portal place. Once you have prepared for this exercise, go to your chosen spot. Lie or sit down with your head in the North or your back to the North. Place air and fire on your left hand, water and earth on your right, in the order given. You may have to practice what we have termed blended consciousness *in other exercises—entering a deeply relaxed and meditative state, but keeping the eyes open—to be able to touch each element without knocking it over or burning yourself.*

Relax, open your chakras, connect and protect. When you are relaxed, centered and ready, begin.

Think of the metaphysical and psychological qualities given to air. Sense the physical element with your left hand, waving your hand through the incense smoke or holding your hand in the breezes flowing around you if you are outside. Which qualities of air do you have? Which are you lacking in that you would like to have? Are there negative attributes of air that you would like to balance or mitigate? Meditate on these thoughts for a few minutes.

Continue with the physical element of fire. Sense the heat of the flame with your left hand. If you are outside on a sunny day, take in the warmth of the sun. Ask yourself the same questions: which qualities of fire do you have, do you lack, do you wish to balance?

Repeat this procedure with the elements on your right hand now, first water, then earth. When you have meditated on each and the gifts or drawbacks you feel each element represents in your character, lie or sit quietly.

Feel the presence of all four elements around you. Sense the harmonious combination of the four with yourself in the center. Drink in that sensation. Experience the harmony and balance in your body, deep within yourself. Let it resonate to your core. Remember: you are the microcosm of the macrocosm. As you seek to create balance in the environment through magic and healing for Gaia, you can create balance in yourself, and vice versa. This loop to and from Gaia is always with you.

Think now of how you can bring in more of whichever element you are lacking, or how you can harmonize with the one dominating in you. For example: are you very "heady" and cerebral? Perhaps an air sign in the zodiac (Aquarius, Gemini, Libra)? Try more sports and physical activities, more hands-on projects. Use your physical environment to help, too. For example, it may help you to stay grounded if you have regular exposure to Nature, to plants and animals. Burn candles and surround yourself with brown, green, purple, orange, red, and yellow.

Do you feel you are impulsive and quickly angered? Are you quick to act but slow to follow through or commit? Could you find calming techniques for your temper through mental techniques, such as counting or breathing deeply, or through meditation and diet changes? Remind yourself to stop and think before making any decisions. Avoid red or orange in your home; use blues of all shades, pale pink, soft yellow, darker earth tones. Play soft music and maybe run a little tabletop fountain as a soothing influence.

After you have fully considered the sides of yourself that might need balancing and the elemental ways that might provide harmonizing aspects, prepare to end the exercise. Close your chakras with a visualization or by eating or drinking.

You can continue to use this exercise for personal exploration throughout your life. Continually seek balance and harmony in yourself as a healing tool, both for yourself and for Gaia.

We have connected more intimately with the Elements around us and in our own personalities, but we've worked with them on the purely physical level. Let's move in to a more metaphysical dimension, to meet the Guiding Spirits integrally involved with those physical elements.

First Acquaintance with the Watchtowers

Every tradition will have its own visualizations to go along with how it conceives of the Guardians or Rulers of the Watchtowers. In some traditions, these Elemental rulers have different names and may all be male; in others, they are both male and female. My tradition uses a specific visualization connected to each of the Guardians of the Watchtowers, who guard the Circle.

Beyond connecting with Earth herself and with the Elements in Nature, it is vital that each member of a coven or participating group be very familiar with the specific visualizations used in his or her tradition. All members should be able to immediately visualize the same images for the Elemental rulers. Common specific Elemental symbols and rulers' manifested appearances are essential in the magic Circle in order to have a cohesive "group mind," that pool of consciousness linking the participants.[5] This enables the group to project a powerful magical force as a whole.

While different traditions have differing systems of names and even of genders for the Elemental rulers, we will use only the Gaia Group and Temple of Gaia system here so as not to confuse beginning practitioners.

Male Elemental Rulers/Symbol	Female Elemental Rulers/Symbol
East: Paralda—air/circle	West: Nixsa—water/crescent
South: Djinn—fire/triangle	North: Ghob—earth/square

The following exercise will aid in building a familiarity and ease in working with these specific manifestations of the Elements and their rulers.

Exercise 17: Meeting the Elemental Rulers

Prepare with a relaxation exercise and a chakra opening.

You are standing on a high mountain. It is very early morning, just after sunrise, and the wind is blowing pleasantly around you. Birds are swooping through the clear morning air, and as you focus on them, you see that they are huge hawks or perhaps eagles. Before you stands a great fortress made of a light-colored stone; its gateway, directly in front of you, stands open. You feel drawn to it and begin to walk toward it. As you reach the gate and enter through the tall stone archway, a figure appears, a young man, walking toward you. As you approach one another, you come into a huge hall in the fortress. There you meet the slender, ethereal, blond man, and you see that he has a golden crown on his head. His clothes are billowing, shimmering shades of orange and blue with a silvery white tunic. On his chest he wears a medallion with a circle engraved on it. The Lord of Air smiles at you regally but kindly and bows slightly in a genteel manner; then he gestures to you to return to the gateway with him. As you walk along you see that he also wears a huge sword at his side. Together you walk out to the mountainside again and stand watching the day brighten and the eagles fly overhead. Commune with him for a few moments and become acquainted. Now bid the Lord of Air farewell and turn to walk down the path ahead of you.

The stony path leads down the mountainside. You find the descent easy and soon you come to a valley. As you walk along, you see a beautiful forest in the nearby distance. You walk toward the forest, and soon you notice a great palace in the middle of the trees. The sun has climbed high in the sky; it is nearly noon. As you approach the palace, you discover that it is constructed of a bright orange red stone. An older man with fiery red hair comes out of the palace. As he approaches, you notice his green and red tunic, covered by a diaphanous cloak of yellow. On his head he wears a golden crown made from three triangles, and in his right hand he carries a tall staff. You approach each other just outside the palace, and he smiles warmly and salutes you with a raised hand. He too wears a medallion, but this one has a triangle engraved on it. The sun beats hot on the stones surrounding the palace, and little, agile, multicolored salamanders play between them. The Lord of Fire invites you to sit on a bank next to the palace wall. Sit and commune with him for a bit then bid the Lord of Fire farewell. You walk out of the palace yard toward the trees and enter the forest.

You stroll happily through the great sun-streaked forest as the day grows late and the sun lowers in the sky. You can hear birds and small animals going about their business, and the forest has a sense of harmony in it. As the shadows lengthen and twilight nears, you come to a clearing in the forest. Ahead you see a mound or knoll that rises on the bank of a great body of water, perhaps a lake or a river or ocean. As you approach the water, a woman appears out of the darkening shadows and climbs onto the knoll, stretching out her arms to the sky. A full moon is rising in the sky, and she seems to be offering the moon a chalice of silver. You stop to take in the beauty of the scene, and the Lady turns to face you. Your presence does not surprise her, and she greets you with her arms outstretched. You approach her and she steps down from the knoll to meet you. She is a beautiful young woman in a flowing black and white gown. She wears a cloak of green edged with designs of white sea foam. On her long, dark hair sits a silver crown with upward-facing crescents. Stroll with the Lady of Water under the moon. As you walk, notice the many creatures swimming and splashing in the moonlit water. Walk with the Lady awhile and get to know her.

Eventually, bid the Lady farewell and continue on. The path leads back into the woods. The moonlight helps you to see, casting shadows and brightening all. Soon the woods give way again to open land, and you see that this is cultivated land, full of crops nearing harvest. The night grows on and soon the stars begin to twinkle out as a hint of dawn comes. The birds begin to twitter and chirp as daylight approaches. As your path rounds a bend, you discover a great throne on a rise in the next field. As you approach the throne, you realize that from it you can see for miles in the distance; a wide river snakes away—perhaps the same water you walked near earlier.

Now you see another woman walking up the opposite side of the rise, a short but stately older woman. She climbs to the throne in a dignified manner. As she sits, you notice a small child sitting on the ground beside the throne and playing with rabbits, squirrels, other small animals.

They all see you and greet you without any alarm or surprise. You climb the rise and join them. The Lady, robed in yellow and purple, holds a great Pentacle on her lap. Her blond hair has gray in it, and she wears a crown encircled by four squares. She reaches her hand toward you, and you sit at her feet. Commune with the Lady of Earth and her companions for a bit.

Finally, you must leave the Lady of Earth. Bid her and her companions farewell and return to the path. As your feet touch the dirt path, let your consciousness drift back to your body, back to physical sensation and the sounds that surround you here.

In your own time, open your eyes. Ground yourself once more with a chakra closing or by eating or drinking.

You will work with these Elemental rulers constantly in your craft of healing and projecting energy. They are your consummate allies and helpers in magic. In a later chapter we will explore the importance of developing a relationship with the Gods. However, the relationship the Witch, Wiccan, Magician, Shaman, or any practitioner of Earth Magic and Earth Healing has with the Elementals is *fundamental*. Practice this pathworking as often as needed to feel at ease with these beings. Treat them with respect and deference. You should be able to visualize them very easily and clearly, even with your eyes open.

Working with the Elementals with your open eyes employs the same skill we practiced earlier with seeing auras and learning to maintain a deeper level of consciousness. There are so many occasions when we must maintain a kind of blended consciousness—keeping a near-trance state while moving through a ritual, performing practical, mundane-plane tasks. Such a technique takes years of practice, but as the much-quoted expression from the Tao Te Ching says: "The longest journey begins with a single step."

Explore different traditions' relationships with the Elemental rulers and find which form or manifestation fits best for you. Some traditions in the style of "High Magic" or "Ceremonial Magic" call upon the Archangels to be the Watchtower rulers of the different elements. We will not go into that style of working here; however, it bears mentioning.

As Healers of the earth we must learn to work harmoniously and respectfully with these various powerful beings. Like the mammals, reptiles, birds, fish, insects, and other life-forms with which we share our planet, they are our companions and fellow travelers. For example, it would be remiss to not mention the common Pagan and Wiccan practice of talking to flowers, herbs, trees, and other plants before cutting or harvesting them. You may wish to ask permission first, which prepares the plant and its guardian Elemental. Of course, it is also important to thank the plant for the gift that you are taking. If you absolutely must cut down a tree, which for a Pagan or other Earth-honoring practitioner is a very significant act, first honor that life with a ceremony of some kind. At the very least, cut it down mindfully and with appropriate solemnity.

As we coax the Elementals out of their hiding places and "caverns deep," convincing them that humanity has not forgotten them and is worth their attentions, your relationship with them will add color and nuance to your life in shades infinitely rich and magical. Never forget, the Elementals are supreme allies in this huge but inexpressibly rewarding task of spiritual Earth Healing and Earth Stewardship. They are a closely related part of our family on Mother Gaia. Talk to them, and then listen well. As Mother Gaia will, they will respond.

Gaia Goals

- Go to your Portal place, if you can, and make an offering (biodegradable, of course) of food, drink, flowers, or cornmeal and tobacco (if you'd like to touch on Native American traditions). You might like to consecrate the offering with some special energy of blessing or protection before leaving it.

  Make sure the place is clean and well cared for. Find out if it is under any kind of threat (of development, etc.) and work to protect it, with political activism and also with magical.

  Honor the earth and the Nature spirits through buying and eating organic, local products.

- Buy organic foods and drink as often and wherever you can. Pesticides cause irreparable damage to your health and to Nature's.

- Support your local farmers and dairy producers. Practice dual conservation by buying foods that come from within 500 miles of your home.

☀ Support farmers who protect habitat and farm organically and consciously. Contact them and let them know your thoughts and concerns. (If you know them well, perhaps share some of your knowledge of the Elementals and Nature spirits. It could help them in their farming!)

Re-examine your relationship with food and with your body. Remember you have blessed yourself as a magical person and a Healer.

☀ Grow and make your own foods whenever you can, organically and with reverence. As is all life around us, food is sacred.

☀ Always remember the concepts you have practiced here of instilling or imbuing a special energy in material things; you can do this with food or drink, too. For example, fill a glass with water and a blessing, and drink it yourself.

☀ As you cook and as you eat, think of the vibration of the food you are preparing or putting in your body. You are a channel for energy—have you cooked your dinner with anger or sadness? What might that do to those who eat it? To yourself? What is the tradition of "saying grace" before a meal but a way of blessing your food, literally? You can change your attitudes about food and become more mindful in how you eat, and thereby nourish yourself on all levels, mind/body/spirit.

Chapter 5
Gifts from the World of Shamanism

I believe that being a medicine man, more than anything else
is a state of mind,
a way of looking at and understanding this earth, a sense of
what it is all about . . .
I've been up to the hilltop, got my vision and my power.
The rest is just trimmings.

Lame Deer, Lakota Medicine Man

The word *Shaman,* generally used for either men or women, is a Siberian word that has become accepted worldwide. Other names over the centuries have included witch doctor, medicine man or medicine woman, sage, wise man or wise woman. All societies have had their version of the Shaman, male or female—whether in the cold polar regions, the misty British Isles, or the humid tropical rain forests. Across the world, on all continents, there have been remarkable similarities in the practices of these mystics and healers from the planet's indigenous societies.

It would be wrong to have a discussion of Deep Ecology and Earth Healing without talking about shamanism and native people's practices, for in a sense the concepts re-emerging in the past thirty years, have drawn much inspiration from the wisdom of the First Nations.

The remarkable mystics known as Shamans lived on the fringes of their communities, taking on the duty of finding answers for the society or individuals. They sought these answers in the spirit world, traveling there—"journeying"—through drug-induced or fasting-induced altered states of consciousness, by extreme physical duress and hardship, or by long years of discipline in trance methods. Typically, rhythmic drumming helped the Shaman reach the spirit world, and the drum was considered the vehicle or horse on which the Shaman "rode." Some sea coast dwellers also used a vision of a boat to travel into that world.

I leave it to indigenous people themselves or to those who have studied directly with the Shamans to teach shamanic techniques. Here I would simply like to share some of the lessons I have taken from my own experiences in the spirit world that could be described as shamanic.

Dancers, Druids, Actors, and Other Human Teachers

Some time ago I studied with a Native American teacher and had the honor of attending a number of retreats, sweat lodges, and dances with this inspiring man. His name is Beautiful Painted Arrow, though he also goes by his "Christian" name, Joseph Rael. He is not a Shaman, strictly speaking, but a Sun Dancer, teacher, and mystic from the Southwestern U.S. tribes, the Picuri Pueblo and the Ute. Educated not only in his tribal ways, but also in the Western world's traditions of academia, Joseph holds university degrees in Spanish and political science.

The kind of extreme personal discipline required for the intensely arduous Sun Dance, or other vision-producing dances and rituals, makes these dancers adept Magicians. They must learn, usually training from early childhood, to transcend this plane spiritually while still dancing, in order to bear the thirst, pain, and exhaustion they experience during the dances. Working with Joseph left a profound influence on my spiritual vision.

Joseph is a superb example of a spiritual activist: his life's work has been to build chambers he calls "Sound Chambers," temples one might call them, half buried in the ground, for the purpose of holding ceremonies dedicated to peace. These ceremonies involve chanting, with music and dance, for the cause of world peace. There are Sound Chambers inspired by Joseph's vision literally all over the earth. He believes that the sound produced in the ground will carry throughout the earth and will change us all. As we discussed in the previous chapter, subtle, simple acts create magic and can heal the earth. The simple act of chanting, the sound permeating the earth and sending vibrational waves throughout Gaia, can make a difference. How important it is to realize that, as we step into the world, conscious, eyes and heart open, our simplest action makes a mark. Joseph's teachings on sound and the spirit world, together with the shamanic techniques I have learned here in the Western United States from other native people and from others who study with Native American teachers, have influenced my views and my practice of Wicca enormously.

Before we learn the technique of "journeying" (and without shamanic training one can only do this loosely and in a Westernized fashion), I would like to point out that those of us of European descent also have a tradition of shamanism in the Druids.

Druidry, as much as we can know of it in the modern world, was a hierarchical Priesthood and Priestesshood of the Celtic people. Since the Celtic society maintained its knowledge and history through oral tradition, the Druids' memories were their libraries and records. When the Celts were converted to Christianity, these traditions were destroyed or driven underground. However, there were many corners of the British Isles where, as happened with Wicca and Paganism throughout Europe, Druidry survived, handed down quietly from generation to generation. Certainly the heredity of the Druids resonate and echo throughout Western society. As Philip Carr-Gomm, Chief of the Order of Bards, Ovates and Druids in the U.K., writes in *The Druid Tradition:*

> The Druids and the power they wielded lie at the roots of our civilisation. These roots are buried. Most of us are unaware of them—believing that our foundations lie instead in the Judaeo-Christian heritage. . . . For the past twelve hundred years or so we have built layer upon layer over our Druid heritage, until it has been forgotten by the majority of us.

He exhorts us to remember this heritage, because our Druidic inheritance can help modern Western society to reconnect with the natural world before it is too late.

Some of the skills the Druids are perhaps best remembered for are their legendary bardic singing and story-telling gifts; they often accompanied themselves on musical instruments such as the harp while recounting detailed heroic sagas. It is recorded that in Ireland the training of a Bard lasted twelve years, by which time he or she had mastered 120 orations, 350 stories, and "the four arts of poetry."

The Druids were also engineers, naturalists, and healers, people who could interpret both the scientific reason behind natural occurrences, and their mystical meanings. To the Druids, as to a Native American, African, Australian Aborigine, or Siberian Shaman, the natural world was alive and peopled with myriad communicative beings. No tree or rock or animal was without a voice and deep significance.

The Druids also had a system for interpreting symbolic significance in Nature. For example, a Druid could explain what a raven flying south, a young deer on a ridge at sunset, or a stone with certain markings might mean. Druids, like Native American Shamans, journeyed to the spirit world aided by rhythmic drumming in order to meet Power Animals.

Another figure we all know, but may not think of as a Shaman, is the actor. The truest forms of acting, the most genuine, transport the audience and actor to the origins of theater, which lie in ceremony and ritual drama. People often think of actors as liars and con-artists and believe that acting is dissembling. I don't know how many times people have said to me, half joking, half serious: "Watch out! You'll never know what she really thinks. She's an actress." However, that could not be more untrue. The art of acting is to portray the *truth* of another human being. Anyone who has studied the great Russian works of Stanislavsky or the Moscow Art Theatre's philosophy or the renowned Actor's Studio techniques knows what a commitment to truth they all demand. Personally I was never as in touch with my feelings and able to recognize what was happening internally, emotionally, psychologically until I had studied acting intensively for some years. Years ago, while far from the wilderness in the heart of New York City or London, acting studies helped me to access and reach my "wild self," my intuitive, genuine self.

In the ancient world, theater was rooted in ceremony and ritual drama, and actors were Shamans and Priests or Priestesses. They used their considerable powers to enter and portray the mind and heart of their characters—thus becoming part of the reality of other beings. The actor today faces the same task—to find the truth of a character and making him or her come to life for the audience. In this sense, all actors are visionaries. The more seriously the performer takes the art and responsibility of portraying the truth of another's experience, the more elevated his or her magical abilities become, and the closer she or he will come to the origins of theater in classical ritual drama and grand mythos.

The British scholar and psychologist Brian Bates, in his book *The Way of the Actor,* asks some of the recent decades' finest actors in Europe and America how they enter into the minds of their characters. Many of their responses sound like a Shaman's description of trance work, of losing oneself inside another being, of "shape-shifting." They bring back from other realms a message desired by the community. I don't think it's a coincidence that the prejudice and distrust shown actors and artists is similar to that experienced by Witches and Shamans. The work they do is messy, scary, emotionally confronting. Perhaps rather like being a Shaman at the edge of society.

Of course "ordinary" people can be our teachers, too. It is easy for activists to develop a jaundiced attitude toward their fellow humans. Indeed, it is often a challenge to honor our fellow humans, when, as ecologists, we may blame our own species for the degradation befalling the planet—but love and accept them in all their myriad diversity we must. After all, we are all children of Gaia. If we can't resonate with our own species, how can we expect to resonate with nonhuman creatures? As Gary Snyder wrote: "A properly radical environmentalist position is in no way anti-human."

For the most part, however, we humans are remarkably unobservant. We tend to see *through* others, instead of into them. We often judge by superficial levels of interaction, and discard or discredit the other signals and senses that we all send out through body language, dress, expressions. It takes huge courage to be compassionate and to become committed to healing. It takes courage and dedication to look into the life of another human being, of an animal, or of our planet—and to care.

We have practiced various Deep Ecology exercises in observing how we feel in certain places in Nature. We have experimented mentally in pathworkings to become other people and other beings. We have practiced connecting with objects that are special to us, or that represent special places. Now we will take it all a step further, by challenging our limits of self a little more. Shamans and others who live at the edge of society, like ecologists sometimes, experience many challenging and risky emotions and realizations. Artists, writers, musicians also have to walk "in another's moccasins" to know why people do what they do, or say what they say, in order to create the art they want. We are going to push our usual parameters now a little more outside our everyday lives. In our comfortable Western society, we screen life out that seems too confronting, too stretching, too evocative of emotions we would rather forget. We drive in our cars and trucks, send e-mails, and stay isolated in our homes in front of television rather than "rub elbows" with the world we would rather avoid.

So, for the next exercise, I want you to go out into the world, to a place you wouldn't ordinarily visit, and simply observe people you might not normally meet. Your aim is not to look with a clinical interest, in a cold objective manner, but rather with a subjective, compassionate connection. What you see there may not be pretty or comforting, or even familiar. However, in order to truly become Magicians who work on a global level, we must stretch our boundaries. Heightened powers of observation are a tool we all need in all areas of our lives.

An essential part of becoming a magical activist involves stretching our powers of observation and metering our own reactions to people through the lens of compassion. As early Christianity taught, as the ancient Greeks wrote, as so many world religions and philosophies have shown, until we can learn to truly love ourselves and those around us, we will remain limited individuals. In the Wiccan view, we must act out of love in order to be powerful magically. *The most powerful energy of the cosmos and of Divinity is love.* It is ultimately the All-That-Is. And, like the Gaian healing magic that is our purpose here, the love comes back to us, enhancing our lives and our personal power in a cosmic feedback loop. More evidence is thus revealed of the Karmic Law of Retribution, in a slightly different vein. Try this exercise whenever you have the opportunity. Observe, take in, find your compassion.

Exercise 18: Observing without Judgment

Choose a place in human society that you would not usually go, a place that is somehow uncomfortable, or strange, or confronting to you. Depending on who you are and what your life has been, that can be any number of situations. It might be the opera on an opening night, or a church soup kitchen on a snowy day. It might be a sandwich counter in an impoverished part of your town, or an outdoor market in a neighborhood of a different ethnic group from your own; perhaps a homeless shelter or a trendy café in an elegant part of the city. Ask yourself: "What poses a challenge? What would help me to see people I would usually avoid?" However, please be sure that you are not putting yourself in any physical risk. The point is not to be physically endangered, of course, but to stretch your understanding of other human beings while observing them. Do not be obvious about your watching and do not be intrusive. Be discreet and do not make anyone uncomfortable. Dark glasses and/or a hat may help with that.

Look closely at the people around you. What are they wearing? What kind of clothes, shoes, jewelry? Do they have hats on? How do they style or cut their hair? Can you smell any perfume or other scent? Are they eating; if so, do you recognize the kind of food? How do they eat (hold their utensils, etc.)?

Now observe how people walk or sit or gesture while talking. What signs and signals does their "body language" give you about their state of mind? Are they confident and happy? Angry and defiant? Confrontational? In love? Lost in thought? Can you sense any specific sort of energy coming from them that helps to identify their mood or mindset? What do you observe that offers insight about their philosophical leanings or political beliefs? Do you hear a language other than English? What is it? Can you identify how the people or person you are observing feels about certain things, or how they relate to another in a relationship? Now turn your outward-focused attention inward for a few moments. Take what you have already observed and check on your reactions to it. Does anyone make you uncomfortable? Has something bothered you about the way someone has dressed, or walked, or done their hair, or perhaps about the ethnic/religious/racial group they belong to? Can you identify what it is that bothers you? What feels strange about what you have observed? Is there anything that you really liked? Something that made you smile and that brought a happy thought or memory?

Continue to observe quietly and with outward focus once more. Try not to make any judgments of any kind now. Just watch intently and carefully, as though you were a small child or a visitor from another planet. Let the images and impressions come in, but do not put labels on them. Simply let your internal camera take pictures; record the images and take them on board your psyche.

When you have observed for some time, an hour or more, you may leave to go about your normal life.

In your musings on the people you met, or watched, or walked around, keep the image of the web of life in your mind. In mapping the human genome, science has recently discovered that the DNA of human beings is 99.9 percent alike. This means that on the genetic level, there is nearly no difference among humans, despite differences in race, color, stature, hair, eyes, and so on. Whether standing in the Kalahari Desert of Africa observing tribal dances, eating yak cheese in an animal-skin tent in the Himalayas, or mingling with wealthy New Yorkers at a Broadway theater, people are tied together in spirit as children of Gaia.

Animal Teachers

In our culture, people are very tied to their pets, their companion animals. Perhaps you are a pet person. Some people describe themselves as "a dog person" or "a horse person" or "an animal person." Often people feel about their pets as they feel about their families; in some cases, pets even take the place of children, spouse, or extended family. Americans spend an exorbitant amount of money each year on their pets—for food, luxuries, and medical treatment that people in the Developing World could only dream of. This is just one of the reasons many environmentalists do not approve of keeping animals as pets.

Another has to do with the slaughterhouse industry and its appalling record of cruelty toward animals and the grotesque amount of waste and pollution it generates. Slaughterhouses work intimately with the pet food industry. Pets such as dogs and cats also create a huge amount of waste, as anyone who has had a companion animal or who has used a trail where dog owners have not cleaned up after their animals can tell you. Then add to this the destructive multimillion dollar trade in endangered animal species, which are smuggled for pet stores and animal mills. This underworld pet trade is closely allied with criminal rings involved in smuggling drugs and arms, and with much the same ethos of cruelty and violence. These are all powerful arguments.

However, despite my feelings on the environmental and ethical issues around keeping pets, I know that life would be so much poorer without our companion animals. Animals offer humans "windows of consciousness" that allow us to see into other realms of mind and spirit. They, in their amazingly accepting way and with their unconditional love, offer us glimpses of other perceptions of the world. They are some of the best teachers we can have in the pursuit of compassion and interconnectedness. Our pet friends are also often gifted healers—to us and to other beings. Doctors and scientists have observed time and again the healing aspects of spending time with animals for those who are depressed, autistic, ill, or elderly. I suppose the answer to the pet debate is to be as mindful as possible in how we acquire and care for our companion animals, to make their impact on the environment less weighty. For instance, rather than buying an animal from a pet store, first examine if it is possible to adopt one from another family or from an animal shelter.

Animals of all species, domesticated and wild, can offer a kind of Portal to us, a connection to the Animal Kingdom of the Shaman. They are a link to our own wild selves. I do not refer now to only pet species, but to all species. Just as observing humans with an attitude of compassion can lead us to deeper wisdom and knowledge about our human family, it is important to spend time observing many animal species and developing insight and compassion from them.

As we practiced observing people with whom we might not otherwise associate, observing animals we don't usually see can be a great lesson and opportunity for growth. Here's an example that touched my life and taught me a valuable lesson recently. My family of four humans and two nonhuman mammals recently grew to include two pet rats, common rats of the species *Rattus norvegicus*. That species classification means that they look like the rats I used to see in the New York subways and back alleys—large gray brown rats.

When I told people about my son's new companion animals, many adults reacted with horror: "Yuck!" "I hate their tails!" "I can't look at them!" "How can you stand them?" Do these reactions come from memories stored deep in the collective unconscious of the fearsome plagues suffered again and again in Europe? Or is it a squeamishness about hygiene? Wild rats have, for centuries, eaten people's food stores and left droppings, while also spreading fleas, another source of disease. No doubt they have been a scourge of pioneers, farmers, and seafarers over the centuries. But I have to admit, my loyalties have been completely taken by our two rat friends. They might evoke feelings of loathing in some people, but they offer gentle curiosity and affection.

Rats are actually clean, intelligent, and extremely companionable animals, as many scientists who work with them in laboratories have discovered. (In fact, animal welfare journals frequently carry articles about scientists who have developed unexpected attachments and affections for the animals they are using in their experiments, and rats are one species often mentioned.) It has been a great delight having the opportunity to observe and learn more about this much misunderstood species.

Ancients of the world have taught through parables, stories that conveyed the lesson they sought to demonstrate. Many parables or fables, like the well-known ones of Aesop, use animals and their unique attributes to teach. The Chinese horoscope illustrates the gifts, skills, and lessons for each human through the animal assigned to the year they were born. Native American lore is filled with animal teachers and animal parables. Even the creation myths of certain tribes involve animals giving birth to the world.

We humans have tended too often to give human characteristics to animals, unfortunately. We anthropomorphize them, making them into humans with fur or scales or shells or wings. In doing so, we fail to recognize the intrinsic value of the animal, totally separate from whatever similarity or lesson or concept it offers to humanity.

Henry Beston wrote in *The Outermost House*, a classic of American Nature writing:

> In a world older and more complete than ours, they move finished and complete, gifted with extensions of the senses we

have lost or never attained, living by voices we shall never hear. They are not brethren, they are not underlings; they are other nations.

Other nations—a powerful thought. As nations, animals should experience the sovereign rights that we award nation-states. It is not necessary to humanize or anthropomorphize animals in order to treat them justly or to endow them with rights. It is enough that they are members of our earthly family, like so many beings, and therefore are deserving of respect and rights. As Earth Magicians and Earth Stewards, we can make them part of our ministry. The huge benefit that this close alliance and companionship offers us in return is the chance to peer through other species' eyes in our daily lives, to perceive another species' view of reality.

I encourage you to spend some time observing an animal you do not know or understand. Ask yourself: "How can this animal teach me? How can knowing and observing it heal me? How can I aid or give back to this animal?" The exercise will help you to grow more connected to our family here on Mother Gaia. Additionally, as you will soon discover, you never know what kind of Power Animal might appear to you. Try to stay open-minded to the gifts and lessons that all animals can teach.

Meeting Your Power Animal

As we discussed earlier, the land that a person calls home will add its unique flavor and form to the kinds of communication that person has with the earth, the Elementals, and the Gods. A person who is open to the spirit world and in communication with the forces of the land could not help but be influenced by the magical energy left by those who have gone before. How could you, for example, live in Australia and not feel the call of the Dreamtime, practiced by the indigenous tribes of Australia? Or live in Africa and ignore the awesome power of the ancient Gods worshiped there? Or in the British Isles, how could one not feel the magic in the ancient oaks standing through centuries, or the animals unique to its shores. I never encountered a bison or coyote or bear in my Circles in the U.K. and Ireland, but I did see many a stag, hare, frog, and dolphin, and even a hedgehog.

Getting in touch with our animal teachers leads naturally to a discussion of "Totem" or "Power Animals." These come to us from the unique international body of wisdom and of spiritual practices lumped together under the term *shamanism*. Power Animal is directly related to the role this being plays in the development of your personal power, or "medicine" as some American Indian tribes call it.

Many indigenous groups believe, for example, that a Power Animal comes to a child early in childhood, and that if one does not, the child will not live long. Many native people also believe that illness is directly related to how whole and complete your power is and whether you have your Power Animal with you. If a person becomes sick, this tradition teaches that the illness might have come about because the person neglected his or her Power Animal. It is important to keep that relationship alive and growing—like the relationships we create with the Elemental rulers. In the next exercise, you will meet your Power Animal.

Exercise 19: Meeting Your Power Animal

The shamanistic world consists of an underworld, a middle world, and an upper world. Generally when the Shaman goes to meet a Power Animal, a Totem or helper, he or she travels into the underworld. It is a mystical place of mythical beings and powerful messages for our healing and well-being.

Think ahead of time of a place where you might descend into the earth—a cave opening, a hollow tree stump, a lake. If you have a real place in mind, one that you know in your everyday life, it may help in the first sessions of this pathworking. This is a Portal that will lead you into the underworld—another plane of existence. However, it is important to mention that you must never compromise your personal safety by going into human-made portals, such as mine openings or tunnels. Instead, sit just outside the opening and visualize going into it.

The purpose of this meditation is to meet the animal spirit that is your personal helper and guide. The Power Animal is very significant in each person's life—even for health and vitality. You should be open-minded to whatever form of animal you may see. Oftentimes the animal or being we meet in the underworld bears no resemblance to the animal we would have imagined as our Power Animal.

Begin with the relaxation exercise practiced earlier, and continue with the chakra opening. You may choose to do the rest of this exercise to the sound of drums, either from a tape or with a friend drumming for you. The drum helps to create the trigger for your unconscious mind. Music can also do this for you with practice. Certain music will help you to shift consciousness right away. I have worked so much with both that either drumming or certain types of instrumental music bring me to trance state very quickly. However, you do not have to have either to reach a trance or deep meditation—silence is good too! You will have to experiment to see which works best for you.

When you are ready, visualize the opening into the earth you have chosen to work with: a cave opening, a tree stump, a lake. Walk to it now.

Go through the opening and begin walking down a long tunnel into the earth. Feel the sides of it—are they smooth? Wet? Rocky? What does it smell of? Earthy smells? Do you hear sounds? It is neither an unpleasant place nor totally unfamiliar. In fact, this tunnel is a place you have experienced before. Move along it toward the end, where you see a light appearing.

As you emerge from the tunnel, you find yourself in a twilight-lit open space. It looks like a great open plain, with meadows and streams stretching away toward the horizon. Off to one side you see a forest in the distance. Near the entrance to the tunnel, you discover an ancient stone seat. Sit down on it and observe the area around you.

The twilight lingers with a silvery gray light. Birds sing their evening songs as they settle down for the night in the distant trees. Bats begin to swoop through the air, and you feel rather than see the silent passing of an owl overhead. This is a place of raw animal power and of ancient mystery. It is a place of many beings, some you may never have seen before. It is also a place that holds the answers you seek.

You have asked to meet your Power Animal. And you now perceive that you are not alone. Let your awareness expand and discover who has come to meet you. Remember to be open to whatever comes to greet you. Not all Totems take animal or bird shapes—you may meet a helper in some other form.

If you sense any threat or danger, if the being you meet seems menacing in any way, you may simply turn and go back up the tunnel. The Portal is not available to these underworld beings. Know that you are safe and you may end the pathworking at any time.

Commune for a time with the being you have met. If it feels appropriate, take a small trip with this being . . . a ride, a walk, a run, even a flight.

When you are finished, thank him or her for helping you and ask if you may meet again.

Then return to the tunnel. Walk slowly up toward the golden light you can see at the top, and emerge back into this world. Slowly come back to awareness of the room around you. Close your chakras down first, or eat or drink to ground yourself again.

Remember where you saw the Portal to the underworld. If it worked well for you, keep it as your place of entry when you want to journey to the underworld again. At first this may be the only place where you meet your Power Animal, although eventually you will learn to see your Power Animal in other places. If you didn't find your Power Animal, then search out another Portal and keep experimenting till you find the right one.

When you meet your Power Animal again, ask how you can best serve the earth. Ask to know how you may do good work and give something back to the planet.

In the Gaia Group and the Temple of Gaia, we stress working on both the mundane plane and the astral plane. Remember: if your Portal is a real place in Nature, honor this place by helping to protect it, by keeping it clean. Pick up any trash that has been left there, leave offerings of food or drink, protect it from development.

I am blessed with having a number of wild places in my life where I have met Elementals, guardian animal spirits, and the spirit of Nature. Some of these precious spots are from my childhood in the Hudson Valley of New York State. Some I have encountered as an adult here in North America or when abroad in the U.K., Europe, South or Central America. I have learned recently that a couple of the Portal places I have been drawn to in New York State and Colorado are unofficially Native American sacred sites. Indeed the power of the energy at these places is palpable, as one would expect in a place that has been honored for centuries. One place dear to me in Colorado is in the wild San Juan Mountains. I have used this spot for journeying and pathworking many times. A few years ago, while visiting there, this message sprang to mind, nearly fully formed.

Mountain Heartbeat

I am the Spirit of the Mountains;
I am She who walks with the Wind.

I am the great puma on silent feet,
observing unseen on rock ledges.
I am the she-bear with cubs
who pauses, sniffing the breeze.

Man hears my call,
but does not know Me;
Man senses my heartbeat,
but does not respond to Me.

I am the blinding blizzard,
the avalanche and the ice storm.
I am the high country tundra,
fragile carpet of jewel-like flowers.
I am the crystalline rock face;
I am the igneous remnant of a volcano's molten blood.

Call me Grandmother Spirit of
Wolf Medicine, "La Loba";
Wolf walks here no more, but I do.
Come sit by my fire, if you dare,
and I will teach you my forgotten ways.

Run on my high plains,
gallop my wind trails
and walk my deep forests;
leap rock to rock in rushing mountain streams.

I am the piercing hawk wind of winter,
whistling in frozen pines like distant thunder.
I am the Wild Heart of the Rockies.
I will beat with you, O Human creature,
but not for you.

Hear Me, run with Me, honor Me.
I am the Spirit of the Mountains;
I am She who walks with the Wind.

We have used this poem in ritual in my coven a number of times since
it first came to me. Giving voice to these words adds to their power. As
part of your Earth Magician/Deep Ecologist training, I recommend that

you try speaking them aloud. Take note of what you feel or see or dream later.

Shape-Shifting

At this point we will return to the work we started in chapter 3, where we began to feel our oneness with the beings around us. This time we'll go deeper, so that we actually feel that we live their experience. This has been called "shape-shifting" by some. Shape-shifting is what the name implies: the magical ability to change one's shape, either in the physical world (very advanced magic, obviously!) or on the metaphysical astral level, to become another being in mind, heart, or body. This ability to connect with animals may be the root of the ancient European legend of the Werewolf, with a sinister twist thrown in to scare or warn children and the unwise.

Feeling this sort of oneness with the living world around us has deep implications for our magic work. *Interconnectedness is the root to compassion, and compassion is the root to the highest spiritual wisdom. This in turn is the key to the most heightened levels of personal magical power.* All life is connected by a great web of energy, and as we learn to sense the movements and vibrations of that vast web, we grow in both compassion and power. Think of the great teachers and mystics. They are alike in the vast compassion they knew. It was the root to their wisdom and their magical gifts.

Exercise 20: Shape-Shifting

Begin again with the relaxation exercise followed by the chakra opening. Surround yourself with protective white light. You should now be able to do this quickly and effectively.

Return to the Portal into the underworld you found earlier. Move down it again, till you reach the opening to the silvery light of the twilight world.

As you emerge from the tunnel, you realize you no longer walk on your two legs. You have metamorphosed into another kind of animal as you traveled down the tunnel.

Do you have legs? How many do you have? Four? Two? Eight? What kind and how long are they? Do you have fur? Or scales? Do you have skin, or a shell? Do you have wings? What kind of vision do you have through your new eyes? Is your sense of smell extremely acute? Do you have a new language? How does it sound?

Live this experience of being inside another's body. Live it intensely. Fly through the air on your new wings, or crawl across the ground on your new paws; swim under water and breathe if this body allows it. Sit and look around at the world, perceiving it in this creature's way.

After a time living this being's life, return to the tunnel. Before entering, thank the body you have had for this experience. Thank any teachers or guides or companions who came along.

Begin to travel back up the tunnel to the world of your everyday life. Bring your awareness back from deep relaxation and return to your own body. Remember to close your chakras down first, or to eat or drink something.

There are many other helpful techniques for gaining wholeness and personal health in the shamanic world. If this is an area that your soul resonates to, I recommend that you read Michael Harner's works or others' writing on shamanism, and that you look for a teacher who can work with you personally. There are many, many gifts that can be found in this realm of study, from whichever part of the planet you may choose. And there are many ways of giving gifts back to Gaia and to our fellow beings through this particular path of magic.

❃❃❃❃❃❃❃

Gaia Goals

Our nonhuman companions have so much to teach us, on the astral and the physical planes. Exercise your compassion, your Earth ethics, and your buying power to help them.

- Can you adapt your diet to semi-vegetarianism, or perhaps some days of the week eat completely vegetarian? Even vegan?

- Do you know how responsibly or ethically the household or personal products you use were made? A good website for finding out who tests their products on animals and who doesn't is www.peta.com for People for Ethical Treatment of Animals (PETA). Or call them in Virginia, USA, at 1-757-622-7382.

- Vote with your buying power! Contact the companies who make the products you like. If these companies use animals for testing, let them know you will stop buying their products till they stop testing. PETA gives addresses for many companies who make common products.

☀ Volunteer with a local animal organization or shelter. Such organizations need help of all kinds! Also donate to them—money, used blankets, cages, pillows, pet toys, leashes. Buy some extra animal food when you are in the supermarket and donate it.

☀ Hug a tree or a rock; get reacquainted with a plant. Mentally send them a hello or a warm greeting. What might you hear or envision or learn in response?

Also put your compassion toward fellow humans into action.

☀ If you are in the United States, is there an Indian reservation near you in need? If you are in Africa or Asia or the Pacific Rim, is there a place to offer aid to the native people who may be less well-off than you?

☀ There are various excellent organizations helping tribal people to preserve their integrity, their sovereignty, and their native ways of life. One such group is Rainforest Action Network (www.ran.org); another is the fine Earth Island Institute (www.earthisland.org; 300 Broadway, Ste. 28, San Francisco, CA 94133; 1-415-788-3666). A superb international organization working specifically for tribal people is Survival International, in the U.K. and other countries (www.survival.org.uk or www.survival-international.org).

☀ And never forget to spread blessings with your magical activism— you can protect and heal through the astral too.

Chapter 6

Transformation through Crystal Magic

The fundamental conception of magic is that of
the spiritual vitality of all nature.

T. W. Rolleston

We who work magic do it through shaping and transforming energy. As
you have already begun to practice, we use our own energy field, our
bodies' subtle energy power centers, and the chakras, as well as the planets' magnetic energies. In ritual we call upon various Deities to help us,
and therefore we work with Divine energy also. Some would say that the
two are not separate—the energy flowing through our bodies to us from
the earth and the cosmos is Divine—it is only the name that changes.
Many of those known as Witches have been healers from time immemorial, utilizing the natural resources and energy sources that abound,
though seem to be hidden to some.

Here I'd like to discuss how crystals can tie in to our work as Healers
and Deep Ecologists. Crystals contain different elements relating to
earth, air, fire, and water. In fact, in a certain sense, the composition of
crystals could be said to be similar to our own. Of course crystals are silicon dioxide–based, with other components, while humans are largely
carbon- and calcium-based. However, the human body broken down
into powder and liquid would leave enough minerals and water to half
fill a bathtub. These similarities cause us to be very compatible companions. They also lead to the most significant reason why crystals make
powerful tools and magical helpers: *crystals have the ability to balance,
harmonize, project energies, and raise vibrations.* Why would it be more
thrilling and powerful to pray with Grandma's rose quartz rosary than
a plastic or glass one? Sentiment? Beauty? Yes, but also because of the
energy stored—from years of absorbing and projecting Grandma's
prayers—and emanating from the quartz beads.

Unfortunately the crystal-wearing boom of the 1980s and '90s made
them seem tacky and even silly. People started touting crystals' healing
powers to the inexperienced and untrained, adding to the public's

skepticism. Happily for the earth and for the stones themselves, it seems as though the super-trendy commercial interest in crystals has begun to wane. Now those of us with a true interest in the stones, in their fascinating makeup, and in their uses for energy projection and healing can quietly go about it. For those of you who have any lingering reticence about crystal healing, a discussion of the scientific theories about the established properties of crystals may help to dispel your skepticism. For those who do not have any set negative impressions, this discussion can simply add to your knowledge about the history and properties of crystals.

Geology, Physics, and Metaphysics

Years ago when I was preparing a talk on crystals for a large Wiccan conference in Europe, I came across the following quote in *The Cosmic Crystal Spiral* by Ra Bonewits: "Science is the branch of mysticism that deals with the measurable."

To thoroughly discuss the physics and geology of crystals you would have to talk about the history of the creation of the Universe, all the planets in our galaxy, the sun, our moon, and most of all, of the earth. Then you'd have to look at the evolution of humanity as well. Of course I'm not going to do that here. However, it's important to know a few bits of science to get the big picture, and the big picture of crystals is truly big.

First, some fundamentals about crystals:

- A mineral is an inorganic substance produced by nature that has a specific chemical makeup and a specific chemical structure.
- A crystal occurs when a mineral solidifies and grows without interference, so that flat faces are produced and arranged in angular, highly ordered, symmetrical shapes and geometric patterns.
- The earth is 99.9 percent minerals, and 99.9 percent of the mineral kingdom is in a crystalline state.

What happens to create these magnificent formations? Molten fluids made up of various mineral compounds flow through some sort of opening in the earth. As they flow along, they deposit dissolved mineral matter. Obviously, it takes very high temperatures and tremendous pressure to mold and melt silicon dioxide. When the minerals are neither crowded together nor disturbed, their flat faces and angles and shapes have room to grow. Seed material must be there at the outset, which then forms layer by layer. As it proceeds without disturbance, the high level of order of the crystalline molecular structure can develop.

This leads us to the physics that create the metaphysics we are interested in. The reason a crystal has flat faces and angles in its outer geometric form is because of the *precise patterns* its molecules make internally. These molecules are composed of silicon and oxygen linked together in a network or pattern called a "lattice." There are only fourteen basic molecular patterns from which all crystals form. Therefore, the physical forms of the crystal's external appearance reveal how it is arranged inside. This once more exemplifies beautifully the ancient Mystery school teaching of Hermes Trismegistus:

As above, so below;
as the Universe, so the Soul;
as within, so without.

This famous law of occult doctrine, manifested in Gaia theory, is again manifested in the crystalline composition of the Mineral Kingdom.

These atomic patterns, or lattices, are energy patterns. Energy occurs in crystals at the atomic and subatomic levels. For a number of mysterious reasons, those fourteen special atomic patterns cause energy to "bounce around" inside the crystals. This means that energy moves along the axis of the lattice in a manner specific to that crystal's structure and makeup, and it is *amplified.*

The result is resonance and vibration. This could be written out as *energy* leads to *resonance* which leads to the *vibratory rate.* Since that resonance is governed by the individual atomic pattern, the flowing, bouncing, and changing depends on the characteristics of that individual crystal. In this sense crystals are very much like human beings: we are similar to one another, sharing many aspects of our physiology and makeup, but each person remains a distinct and magnificently unique individual.

Like crystals and like all living beings, we have a field of electromagnetic energy that vibrates constantly. The difference between the electromagnetic field of humans and that of crystals is that the vibratory rate of crystals is higher, more exact, and steadier than ours. Our rate of vibration ebbs and flows with our moods, health, level of fatigue, diet, tension, and so on. As we have discussed already, it is possible to both raise and balance it in many ways—for example, through exercise, meditation, time in Nature, connection with animals, music, magic, and sex. We can work on harmonizing our vibratory rate with others, such as in the "group mind" of meditational or magical workings together. However, whatever we do, our rate of vibration is still volatile and highly variable.

The crystals' "oscillation"—their pulse of energy or electricity—is known as "Piezo-electricity," which has a *highly precise rate*. This is what makes crystals so unique, highly prized, and essential in electronics. This brings us to the crux of it all—that is, to the gift in the remarkable nature of the crystal, which is to balance and harmonize, to mirror and stabilize whatever energy it comes in contact with. Crystals not only harmonize, but also raise the vibratory rate. *In metaphysical or magical terms, crystals balance your energy and increase your power by heightening your own ability to project energy.* Obviously, this is the key point for our discussion, because the basis of magical workings and healing is the projection of energy.

We could say it is the combination of "Piezo-electricity" and "Pyro-electricity" that causes this effect and gives this ability. Piezo-electricity occurs when the crystal is pressed or squeezed; pyro-electricity means that when heat is applied, polarized changes occur in the electrons at either end of the lattices. When subjected to these influences, or interactions, the crystal's internal structure rearranges itself to match the energy it is exposed to.

Now, let's put it in terms more directly related to our work with crystals. It is conceivable (though not scientifically proven yet) that when you charge your crystal by breathing on it or passing it over a flame, you actually create a pyro-electrical response inside it by causing it to react to the intention you are working for. Similarly, when you hold and squeeze it, you cause a piezo-electrical occurrence to happen within it. There is no doubt to those of us who work with crystals that our interaction causes some kind of internal electrical reaction. I have seen instant reactions in crystals to emotions or intentions. As we will discuss in a moment, I have seen crystals move, by breaking, dropping, or falling off a chain. Strange as it may seem, the intentions sent toward them or the actions happening near them made it apparent that their movement was not accidental or coincidental.

Therefore, when working with crystals, which amplify our intentions and our capabilities, we must be aware that we are working with Earth and her energy on the very deepest molecular levels. We have already begun a practice of projecting energy: to Gaia, around ourselves, into water as a blessing. It is possible to simply work with our own powers of energy projection to perform acts of magic. But if we use the amplification available to us through crystal magic, we must realize the wide-reaching influence we can have. This is why working with crystals is no light or superficial activity, or a cliché about wearing pretty stones or having trendy possessions—at least not for those of higher consciousness and deeper awareness. Don't make the mistake of not taking the crystals seriously. Some even see crystal magic and healing as carrying a fairly heavy sense of responsibility with it ... perhaps even a karmic load. And indeed it does, for as the magical arts teach, all magic is ethically bound and can carry karmic repercussions, both positive and negative.

Use the following pathworking to deepen your acquaintance with the Elemental Kingdom connected with crystals.

Exercise 21: The Crystal Temple

If you have a favorite crystal, or one that you wear regularly, hold it in your hand. If you don't have a crystal to work with, simply hold the image of one in your mind.

Begin with a relaxation exercise and a chakra opening.

You are standing once more at the opening to a large, long tunnel. It can be the Portal you experienced earlier in your shamanic pathworking or another one. The tunnel slopes away, into the ground—or so it appears. You follow it along. There is enough silver light to see where you are walking, and the coolness of the tunnel air feels pleasant. You are drawn deep down along it. Soon you come to an opening.

You emerge easily into a slightly brighter silvery light, which soothes your eyes and gently envelops you. As you look around, you can see a great mountain plain that extends to the horizon.

The plain stretches out on all sides, but is ringed by a continuous chain of mountains, surrounding you. The land rolls toward them with some dips and rises—some almost valleys, but generally a gentle rise and fall to the earth.

As you start to walk toward the nearest rise, you feel the wind blowing gently through your hair, caressing your senses and whispering softly to you. Feel the sensations of the light, friendly breeze as it seems to stroke your skin and enter your every pore. As you walk along you realize that your feet are bare and you can sense the earth beneath them more fully than ever before. The earth has a rich warmth as of a live body. You feel the earth's energies move up your legs, into your pelvis, up through your whole body; the sensations rise through your neck and out the top of your head. It is a pleasure to walk along with this flow energizing you and propelling you along.

You continue to walk toward what appears to be the nearest rise of hills and mountains. Now you see that above the mountains in front of you the sky is glittering with dancing lights. At first it seems to be a volcano throwing off a glow or an aurora borealis dancing in the sky. Then you see that it is emanating from the plateau nearest you.

You approach it steadily, crossing the rolling plain, and you see a long, graduated hill path leading up, up to a beautiful, luminescent structure, an enormous crystal Temple.

Climb to the Temple, up the gently sloping path. The Temple glows more and more warmly with flickering multicolored light from within. As you reach it, you discover a doorway facing you, cut into the stone. The door stands open and you enter. This is a familiar place, a place you know. It feels good to be here.

As you walk into this chamber of crystal, you realize that you are inside your crystal. Move to the center of the chamber and stand, studying the angles of the walls around you. Examine the texture of the stone; touch it; feel it; explore the floor and its many little variations; study each line or curve of the walls, the colors of the stone, how it glows. The stone radiates warmth to you. Look high into the ceiling and search well into the vastness of the chamber's heights.

As you stand there, drink in the Temple's energy, solidity, warmth, space, and light. Now gently become aware of another presence, a being who has joined you inside the crystal Temple.

Commune with this other being. See what messages come to you. It may be a guide, an Elemental, or the Spirit of the crystal itself. Try to find out.

Explore the feelings you receive from the crystal. What feelings do you receive from the being who has come to meet you? After a while, you are ready to leave the crystal Temple. Bid farewell to the presence you have encountered there, and thank it. Bid farewell to the Temple; leave now through the doorway you entered.

Descend the hill path once more to the great plain. In your own time, cross the plain again to the tunnel and come up through it.

Slowly, when you are ready, bring your awareness back from deep relaxation. You may do a chakra closing first, or eat or drink something to close your chakras.

Now that you have communed a little more deeply with a personal crystal, and perhaps met a being from the Mineral Kingdom, let's talk more specifically about how to use crystals in our Earth Healing work.

Earth Healing and Other Techniques with Crystals

It is important, in our work as Deep Ecologists and Earth Magicians, to guard against anthropocentrism, human-centeredness, and to work toward "bio-centrism," life-centered philosophy. Crystals are alive, as the earth is alive, but they do not *experience* life as we humans or other beings do. It is a good practice in our search to widen our circle of compassion and treat crystals with the respect we show to other forms of nonhuman life. Like animals and plants, crystals are made stronger with exposure to sunlight and with water; they need to be treated with care and gentleness. They will literally crack under stress, even emotional or psychological stress.

Let me explain. We Witches and Magicians work with subtle energies, bending and shaping reality through the use of will, visualization, and the power of concentration. As we've seen, crystals are very sensitive receptors of energy, as well as projectors. They will pick up your intention—even if you do not consciously send it their way. That is why, if you are under great stress, a crystal you wear often may respond. Sometimes, for whatever internal reason, they simply cannot tolerate the stress and will react to it either by cracking or by literally getting away from you—for example by falling off a chain or getting lost.

This may sound far-fetched, but I have seen countless examples of this myself. For example, I had a malachite pendant that I loved, and since malachite is very healing to the heart center, I often wore it when I was sad or in need of emotional support. I wore it on a long chain, so it hung right over my heart. The morning after my father died, I decided I had better put my malachite on. Almost instantly the stone cracked and fell off the chain. As I interpret this, either the grief was too strong for it, or it had done its job already in helping me during my father's long illness, and it needed to go on. I thanked the little malachite for its help, then threw it in the ocean to be regenerated through the healing power of water. The malachite's reaction is only one example of the many amazing reactions I have seen from crystals.

You can, however, clear crystals of unwanted energies. When they first come into your possession and you want to clear them of old energies, you can simply wash them in running water (in a stream or under the tap), and then leave them in the sun and moonlight. Another traditional way of clearing them is to leave them in sea salt for a few days. You need to sense the stone's condition, then decide if it needs "relaxing" and clearing for days or maybe even weeks. Some heavier stones, heavy in the psychic sense, like obsidian, may take longer than others to clear. For those interested in practical applications of various types of stones, please refer to appendix A for a list of stones and their uses.

After the crystal has been cleared, it is time to charge it. "Charging" an object in magic means filling it with will, intention, or power. We worked with this concept already in exercise 7, where we charged water with a blessing. Frequently we can simply "will it" with a clear intention in mind and heart while holding the object or crystal. Another method is to use the breath to literally blow an intention or a spell into a talisman or amulet. Here is a simple method for charging your stone.

Exercise 22: Charging Our Personal Crystal

Center yourself and relax. If it is necessary to sit or lie down, then do so now. Open your chakras or, at the least, be sure that you are mindful of your connection to Divine energy through your chakras.

Use your breath, together with an intention held in your mind. Think of what you wish the stone to help you with, what you want to know about the stone, or any other questions you have. As you hold that intention in your mind, blow on the stone with great concentration, and visualize that thought being transmitted into its center or heart. The heat of your breath will cause a reaction to occur inside the crystal. You are interreacting with the Mineral Kingdom and with a being that has an entirely different makeup, but is still related and allied to you.

Sit with the stone for a little while. Listen for any "answers" you may receive; be aware of any images that come suddenly into your mind. When you feel ready and that your time of communing has been sufficient, thank the crystal for its help or its answers.

Come slowly back to everyday consciousness. Be sure to ground yourself and close your chakras if you had opened them.

It is not necessary to wrap the crystal here, as we did in exercise 12 with the Root talisman. (If that feels right, however, then please do so!) If you charged the crystal to help you in some specific way, then you may want to keep it close to you—on your desk or bedside table, for example. If it is small enough, you can carry it in your pocket. Some people like to wear little bags that hold their crystals and other power objects or talismans over their hearts. Some Native American traditions call these "medicine bags." As mentioned in chapter 5, this sense of medicine is not as we in the Western world know it, but rather the concept of our personal power being our medicine. The objects in the little bag help or augment our personal power, as these helper crystals can do.

Crystals are extraordinary helpers in healing, whether with people, animals, or the world around us. When I have taught my workshops on crystals, people often tell me that someone they want to help does not "believe in crystals," and they ask if it will work anyway. Whether we believe or not doesn't matter. As with spells and prayers, the energy that you send out to aid anyone or anything will help no matter the belief of the receiver. It is *your* faith in the intention that powers your magic. (This will be discussed more in the next chapter under the section "The Witches' Pyramid.") In the case of working with crystals, you have an additional helper in your intention—the crystal will do its job and will work at healing or projecting an intention no matter who believes. Crystals are generous and dedicated helpers. Remember their steady rate of oscillation, discussed earlier? Your crystal friend will be there for you, working consistently and steadily. However, as people who are benders and shapers of reality, as people who believe in the principles of magic, we must treat them with care.

A powerful reason for treating the stones with consideration is that because of their ability to amplify and project energy, they constantly receive and project the energies we direct toward them. Therefore, it is wise to send them only the purest of intentions or energies. Because of the Karmic Law of Returns, when any kind of consciousness is projected out into the world, it will return back into your life as well. Remember that when you begin to experiment with crystal workings, even if you may not believe totally in what you have projected into the crystal, or if perhaps you forget, the crystal will keep on with its job.

Try this experiment: charge a crystal with helping you to remember your dreams and see what happens. Once I asked my helper crystal to aid me in that, to learn more about some problem through remembering and interpreting my dreams. Soon I was waking up every hour during the night! Being normally a good sleeper, I began to wonder what was going on. Finally I remembered that I had charged the crystal next to the bed with the intention of remembering my dreams. I had to laugh and, of course, to thank the crystal. (And yes, indeed, I did begin to remember and learn from my dreams.)

Working with crystals is a marvelous preparation for working with Earth. They are part of her in an integral way—having formed in her heart and womb, one might say. Learning to feel and to know what messages they have in their hearts will start you quickly on the path toward knowing what other forms of life hold and need, and you will learn to communicate more clearly with Gaia. These nonverbal, subtle forms of communication can be some of the hardest to learn as you begin to hone your psychic abilities. However, the previous exercises have started you on this path. Trust your intuition more. If you think you have heard a message from a crystal (or a tree or a guide or whatever), trust that you probably have. Now some people may think that I am condoning mentally unstable behavior here . . . but of course I am not. Always examine with meticulous care the message that has popped to mind. If it seems to answer a question you have posed mentally, or if it refers to a prayer or intention you sent out to the Universe, then it may well be "the small, still voice of God" as one Christian saying goes. If the voice says "Jump out the window! You can fly!" then talking to a therapist or doctor is probably warranted. Always remember the magical teaching discussed earlier: "An it harm none, do what ye will." The admonition to harm none begins with yourself.

Earth Healing Crystals

Combining much of what we've learned so far about crystal magic and healing and Earth Magic, here is a simple act of magic that anyone, experienced Magician or beginner, can work. The full Wiccan Circle casting is given in appendix B, for those who wish to learn it Wiccan-style. However, it is possible to create sacred space in many ways and through many different traditions. You can create sacred space *wherever you are,* simply by bringing a more mindful and reverential awareness to each act. Having a loving and compassionate heart is also important. Remember the marvelous thoughts from Michael Schneider on that in chapter 2, where he said that sacred space is within us. A beautiful quote from the inspiring Buddhist teacher Pema Chodron illustrates that sacred space can be anywhere. She writes:

We are always standing in the middle of a sacred circle. Whatever we might be doing, we are in the center of a sacred circle. It is not something restricted to when you are formally meditating or to when you are in a good frame of mind. It is your life, wherever you are, always standing in the center of a sacred circle. . . .

Joy is very much a product of welcoming everything into the circle of your life, whether it's your own emotions and thoughts and feelings or other people and circumstances. Joy is a product of realizing that you are always standing in the center of a sacred space.

Sacred space begins within us. Outwardly creating sacred space can occur in many ways. Depending on your tradition, you might choose a simple meditation. You might choose to light a candle or burn some incense to raise the vibrations in the space. As we have already discussed, candles and incense can help to provide a trigger for the conscious mind to change levels of awareness. The energies of certain herbs and oils in the incense or candles can send out a blessing, add protection, or dispel negativity. However you choose to do your magic, whether with a style of Wiccan Circle casting, or by creating another tradition's sacred space, focus on projecting the sacred Circle as you feel most comfortable.

Exercise 23: Crystal Magic for Gaia

Choose a crystal that you "resonate" to, one that appeals to you and that you feel drawn toward. If you are performing this as a meditational exercise, begin with a relaxation technique and chakra opening. Be sure to surround yourself with white light and protection. If you are working within a full Wiccan magic Circle, then you will probably have already opened your chakras, and you are protected by the Circle.

Hold an intention of some kind of Earth Healing in your mind. Now take the crystal you have chosen and blow on it, charging it with your breath. As you blow out, keep your intention clear and focused. Visualize a place you wish to heal or revitalize, to send love to, to honor—whatever your wish may be. Ask the spirit of the crystal to help you in your purpose; ask the Elementals and the Goddess and God to help you as well. Pass the crystal over burning incense and lit candles, then touch it with salt and water, all in the name of the purpose you have in mind.

Thank the Elementals and the Goddess and God for their help in this magic.

Now wrap the crystal in a piece of clean cloth and leave it on your altar, or in some special place, undisturbed, for three days.

If you have done this as a simple act of meditation, close your chakras down when you are finished. If it is within a fully consecrated Circle, continue with the Circle and close it when you are ready in the usual way.

Once your crystal has rested and been fully charged for three days, bury the crystal in the earth to disseminate your magical intention through the Earth Mother. Choose a place you love or perhaps wish to help—or both. Maybe this is a gift for your Root site, to thank the guides you met at your personal Portal, or perhaps you simply wish to honor and bless your nearby woods, hills, beaches, or other wild place. If you do not have time or the opportunity to go to another site in Nature, you may bury the crystal in your backyard or garden, or any piece of earth available to you. Gaia will still receive your intent.

Leave the crystal buried as long as you like, permanently if you wish. Or you can dig it up again after a period of weeks or months, to cleanse and use again for some magical purpose.

Perhaps it goes without saying, but this technique of charging a crystal in ritual or in deep meditation is not only for Earth Healing. It can be used for any magical intention, to send energy to a person or for a specific need of some kind. It is a lovely way to send magic or healing to someone. A crystal or crystals, whether in jewelry or simply a stone to carry in a pocket or to keep nearby, charged with your love and the blessing of the Gods and Elementals makes a very meaningful gift. You can wrap it in something attractive, a piece of cloth or a little pouch, before you give the crystal away. And remember, the recipient does not even have to believe! Your blessing or healing will aid him or her even so.

"Keepers of the Flame"—The Atlantis Theory

Some writers have proposed a deep, historic reason that "old souls" may be turned off to crystals. They theorize that a memory may live on in the so-called collective unconscious, that shadowy universal realm where all our unconscious minds interpenetrate, of a role that crystals played in the destruction of the lost continent of Atlantis. Atlantis is thought by many to have been a very advanced ancient culture in the central Atlantic, or some say the South Pacific or the South China Sea, which mysteriously sank into the ocean after some cataclysmic event. It may have been a massive natural phenomenon, such as an earthquake or the oceans rising, or it may have been a cataclysm of human creation.

Who can say definitively? This truly is straying far from the proven into the very misty regions of theory, legend, and speculation. However, we are already well acquainted with the Karmic Law of Returns, which could also be termed the law of cause and effect. Therefore, it should be evident that anyone who abuses the power of the stones for his or her own aims could risk havoc on an elevated global scale. This is what is thought to have occurred in Atlantis, ultimately causing the total annihilation of the civilization. This memory may indeed live on in our unconscious. Or perhaps the memory is stored in certain crystals. If this is the case, then we as Earth Healers and Earth Stewards are the best suited to work with crystals in this new era, because of our commitment to protecting and healing Gaia and to what can be termed "white magic."

Whether or not one chooses to believe ancient legends regarding the destruction of Atlantis, understanding the mysterious power of crystals means we recognize the need to work with the stones wisely, ethically, and judiciously. Likewise, we must work magic wisely, ethically, and judiciously. As we have already stressed about other parts of our lives, whether in our buying habits or our resource use, we must live mindfully, awake to the choices we are making and to the energy we send out. In the final chapter, we will discuss Earth Magic and some specific cautionary tales.

Your dedication to the exercises offered here will be deeply satisfying and renewing as you connect more and more with the web of life. Since crystals are such powerful conduits for energy, you can also begin to send messages to Gaia with their aid. We are truly "Keepers of the Flame" in what is far from being a trendy, pseudo-spiritual, commercial pursuit. We are keepers of many branches of esoteric, hidden knowledge—be it from Atlantis, Egypt, Rome, Africa, South America, the British Isles, or wherever. I have called composting a kind of "kitchen alchemy" and a metaphor in the early chapters of this book. I will talk in the next chapter about Earth Magicians and Stewards as rightful inheritors of the ancient art of alchemy in its full-blown, highest purposes. As keepers of enlightened knowledge, we can become the most effective activists for Earth Healing. Therefore crystal magic is a powerful tool for us. These lovely stones are not only examples of the incomparable beauty in Nature, but they also make powerful allies at this key time in our work for Gaia, for ourselves, and for our fellow passengers on the planet.

Gaia Goals

Remembering the vibrational energy and the magic contained in what you wear or have in your home,

- Find out where your things were produced, manufactured, or grown. Is it sweat shop labor? Are people abused in any way in the manufacture of these products? What are the producers' environmental policies? Be a conscious and a caring consumer. Use your consumer power to make a statement with the household purchases you make.

- What kind of jewelry do you wear? How do gold or diamonds affect your personal energies? Are you aware of the stones you may be mixing together? Are you aware of the energies in any stones you wear or live near? Rethink your relationship with your jewelry as an Earth Magician and Earth Steward.

- Organize a boycott if you feel strongly about a certain company's or store's policies. Managerial policies are changed through the company's economics, through the "bottom line."

- Praise the companies you approve of—through a letter, through an e-mail at their website, through a comment at the store. Talk to your local store managers, and fill out comment cards in your local stores.

- Write your town or city council about "good" stores or "bad" stores. Write the mayor or governor. Keep your government representatives aware of your opinions. Letters do affect policy and legislators' opinions!

- Remember to plant healing crystals around your home or town or county . . . use your new abilities to charge a crystal for each place's specific needs.

Chapter 7
Gaia Alchemists and Activists

The true Magi are those who *live* Magic, and not merely tinker with it.
Magicians are not made, they make themselves.

William G. Gray

In the chapters leading up to this we've talked about ways to connect with the earth, the crystals, our animal spirits, and so on. Earth Stewards, Earth Magicians, Shamans, Witches, Alchemists, Deep Ecologists, Eco-Feminists—I have thrown a lot of terms and names around in this book. It really doesn't matter what you call yourself. To use a familiar slogan: "Just do it!" Get out there—off the sofa, out of the car, and away from the shopping mall—and make a commitment to enlightened activism and magical Deep Ecology.

You don't have to be an Initiate to experiment with some ritual practices, as many solitary Witches and Pagans do. While I do not espouse the path of Self-Dedication and Self-Initiation as the very best, I would not want anyone to feel stalled out or hesitant to grow in Paganism and Wicca for lack of a personal, physical teacher. I have known many committed Pagans who work ritual regularly by themselves, at the full moons (Esbats) and the High Festivals (Sabbats). These good people may choose to do their magic solo because they do not have much free time or because they do not resonate to the idea of working with a group. Others simply may not have found the right group or teacher yet. Always remember that your primary and truest teachers are your inner guides, your Higher Self, and the Gods.

In the same way that small steps in ecology lead to greater environmentalism, the seemingly small act of committing yourself spiritually begins the shift in vibration that leads to greater personal evolution. Magical activism and mundane-plane, everyday world activism must go hand in hand. Since everything we do comes back to us threefold, your magical activism will help to fuel your practical activism and your commitment. It involves a kind of programming and reprogramming of yourself. When you have done a ritual to heal the waters or the lands around your home, for example, you will find it very difficult to not be

conscientious about your recycling or your water use the next morning!
And, of course, your personal activism may go even farther.

Three Ancient Magical Precepts

Before we take the step of Self-Dedication, let's look at three ancient
magical precepts. I always teach these fundamental ideas in classes on
Earth Magic:

>Magical Hygiene
>The Witches' Pyramid
>Group Mind

These precepts will not only make you more powerful, each in itself, but
you will also soon see how the three fit together to make you (and your
coven, if you work with a group) very effective Earth Magicians.

Magical Hygiene

To be the most effective channels we can for positive magical power, we
must keep ourselves positive, healthy, and strong in every sense and on
every level, in order even to attempt to heal or to change reality through
magic.

For clarity, one could say that magical hygiene has two parts: (1) psychic self-defense, or protecting oneself against negativity; and (2) personal "cleanliness" and healthiness on the physical, mental, and psychic
levels, which enhance and strengthen one's psychic and spiritual power.

Volumes have been written on psychic self-defense; all I will say
here regarding this huge topic is that we must remember that *negativity invites negativity*. And negativity, in any sense, from self-destructive
living habits to negative ways of thinking, saps your energies on all levels—including the magical level. People who run covens and who have
participated in them know very well that to have a smoothly running,
effective group, everyone must strive to get his and her own life in order.
That means taking care of all aspects of your life—your body, your
sources of income, and your personal life—if you want to help others.

If we are to be healers on any level, and particularly on such an elevated level as Earth Healing, then we must be positive and strong in
ourselves first. Magic takes a lot of energy, as does healing of any sort,
and we must approach it as an athlete, artist, or performer who cares for
his or her body and skills by keeping in optimum shape. We are, after
all, making ourselves channels for Divine energy, and we must be deserving vessels.

Second, it bears repeating that you must safeguard your energy field, your "aura." As we discussed in earlier chapters, all living things have energy fields, sometimes called auras. We each have our own energy field, the chi, ki, or prana, our vital life force. There are many ways of keeping your aura healthy, generally by healthy living in every sense. However we also need to revitalize ourselves and balance our energies by being outside in Nature *every day,* if possible . . . even if it is just for a short walk in a park or a garden. Starhawk discussed this in her seminal work, *The Spiral Dance,* and suggested getting regular physical exercise and making contact with the elements and Nature. I would go so far as to suggest that you walk barefoot, whenever possible, so as to really connect your chakras with Earth energies. (That is certainly the ideal, but in northern climates I confess I don't always do that.) Safeguarding your magical health and vitality requires much reading, study, discussion, and meditation.

The essential thing to remember is psychic self-defense. We referred to this idea earlier in terms of protecting yourself with white light when meditating or divining and doing ritual within the confines of the sacred Circle. You need to keep unwanted influences and energies from hooking onto you, from "infecting" you and your magic, whether they emanate from the depressed person next to you in the supermarket or from a disincarnate entity attracted by your Circle. Like any Witch or psychically oriented person, I have lots of personal stories of encounters with the spirit world, beginning in my childhood. I have already told the story of my childhood encounters with the ghost who traipsed about in my parents' house. In short, there are many beings around us, both visible and invisible. Some have the purest of intentions, and others may not be so pure and high-minded. Some may simply be mischievous or curious.

Practicing magical hygiene is similar to keeping your immune system strong as the first line of defense against disease. Keeping a healthy aura through good magical hygiene is your first line of defense against psychic attack. Your aura and personal vitality form a kind of barrier to unwanted outside influences, both physical and psychic. We have discussed protection techniques in a number of the exercises. You can begin the protective layering, which connects and protects by keeping your chi strong and your aura healthy, in anticipation of your actual meditation.

In connection with magical hygiene, keep in mind the Karmic Law of Threes (or Law of Returns). Wicca abides by this as a guiding rule for all forms of magic, high and low, and for all thought projection, whether conscious or unconscious. As we have discussed, the law expresses that anything you do comes back to you threefold (this is sometimes more whimsically expressed as "the Boomerang Effect"). Tied together with that rule is the Wiccan Rede. Even in a pursuit that seems as righteous and valid as Earth Healing, we must always be absolutely, 100 percent certain of our motives and intents. Keep in mind that even with the best of intentions, things still may not turn out as you planned. With consistent planning and preparation you will have results . . . and they may surprise you. We are human and therefore not able to foresee every possible outcome. This is an additional reason why ethical, thorough preparations are essential in magic.

The Witches' Pyramid

The Witches' or Magicians' Pyramid is a powerful, ancient secret of the occult magical arts known to the Alchemists and High Magicians of the centuries past. The four-sided pyramid has four equilateral triangles with a square base.

The pyramid is constructed of *will, imagination, faith,* and *secrecy.* It is to be used consciously and on the deeper levels in every act of magic as a foundation and a source to your power.

All four concepts are extremely important, but will is the driving force, the engine you might say, behind your magic. Imagination is the clarity of vision and visualization the practitioner needs to really see in his or her mind's eye what the spell or intention is to accomplish. The more clearly you can send your vision out to the Universe, the clearer your results will be.

The concept of faith is the same as in any religion. You must overcome doubt and left-brain rationalism to make the so-called leap of

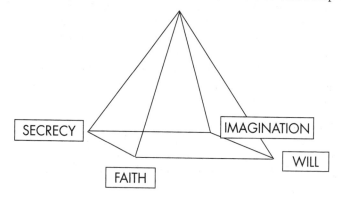

faith. This requires believing not only in your own powers, but also in the power of the Universe to accomplish what may seem impossible. (Remember: "Thaumaturgy" involves accomplishing what are commonly seen as miracles.)

The term *secrecy* has at least two uses in relation to magic. First, people think that those who practice the occult are silent about it because they are doing something wrong or shameful. The word *occult* actually means "hidden," and it refers to the idea that the deeper mysteries of wisdom and knowledge are not for just anyone. It is not that we are elitist but that all people exist at different stages in their spiritual evolution; some may not be ready to learn certain mysteries. Therefore, the mysteries remain hidden or secret until a person becomes ready to seek the arcane knowledge. An ancient Mystery School tenet says: "When the student is ready, the teacher will appear." People must come to certain knowledge and realizations at their own time. When they do, they will be led to the right teachers. I have seen the absolute certainty of this in my own life.

The second use of secrecy in magic that once you have completed a piece of magic, you must not discuss it for a specified length of time. In discussing it, you might second-guess your actions, or perhaps even damage the energy you have created and sent out. If you imagine energy flowing from you and your actions in a pipeline out into the Universe, talking about it prematurely or revising it mentally could poke holes in that pipeline. An old American adage admonishes: "Don't change horses midstream." Reviewing your magical act after you have sent it on its way is a bit like changing horses midstream. Once you've sent it out, leave the vehicle of your magic alone to accomplish its job.

Other traditions have different ways of phrasing these concepts, but the meaning of the Pyramid is essentially the same. For example, some traditions use the words: "To will, to know, to dare, and to be silent." I particularly like the phrasing of "to be silent," since the idea is not that we are hiding anything, but simply keeping silent till the Gods, Elementals, and Universal forces have accomplished what our will set in motion.

Group Mind

In order to do magic of any sort, Earth Healing or otherwise, we must have the ability to concentrate and focus our minds. Through this focusing we learn to become channels through which the force of cosmic energies can flow and be directed, and we learn to connect our consciousness and our will to the limitless store of energy that makes up the Universe. That is the job and should be the goal of each individual. However, even more intimate and direct is what happens to the conscious and unconscious minds of a group when people work intensely together. People connect directly to a certain part of others' minds, which they have "opened" to them, in a manner of speaking. Brian Bates's wonderful study of the world of acting, *The Way of the Actor,* touches on this concept. He quotes the great British actress Glenda Jackson: "There is a curious kind of intimacy that actors have among themselves which is specific entirely to the work. . . . [O]n an acting level you can quite easily break through all those social barriers that keep the world spinning."

I have rarely experienced this "curious kind of intimacy" that goes beyond mere friendship or understanding anywhere except in a cast of actors, a coven, or a family. Perhaps this would be the kind of group thought that existed in early tribal life? The connections made with other people's minds go beyond the bounds of "normal," everyday life. Indeed it is a more primitive, primal means of communication, which would have pre-existed our highly verbal, mechanistic society.

This group mind or pool of consciousness that can develop among people working or living together is absolutely essential for effective magic and effective ritual work. Vivianne Crowley's *Wicca—The Old Religion in the New Age* talks of how "[t]he 'group mind' of the coven exists on the borders of the personal and the collective unconscious. . . . Group magic involves making links between the personal unconscious of one person and another."

It bowls you over when you realize the extraordinary levels on which you can begin to work if you take this a step further: *as we link to the larger group mind of Wicca, we can also link to the larger group mind of Earth Healing.* This is how the development of the group mind enhances and empowers the development of a coven's strength—by linking to the larger, more universal Wiccan "energy stores" of covens and individuals around the globe. And it can become more powerful still.

Consider, if that coven devotes itself in any way to Earth Healing, how much more potent the aid to Mother Earth will be when the magical will of that group mind has accessed the will of the larger, Earth-centered group mind. You can begin to appreciate the power generated by the Gaia Group's World Peace Network of the 1980s, where people performed the same ritual at synchronized times with the intention of bringing peace to the planet. There is the example I gave in chapter 1 of when, in 1990, I discussed the power of such magical workings in Germany with people who had participated in the Peace Network there while I performed the same rituals in New York. We realized the wide-ranging changes that had taken place, culminating in the end of the Cold War. Mikhail Gorbachev had begun implementing perestroika and glasnost in the 1980s, policies that led to the breakup of the former Soviet Union; the Berlin Wall had come down, and Germany had been reunited. A new era seemed to be dawning. Who can say if our magic led directly to these global events? It certainly didn't hurt and could only have added to the groundswell and momentum. However, if James Lovelock is right, and we humans are an extension of Gaia's conscious-ness, then *by linking to the group mind of Earth Healing across the planet, we link it to Gaia directly.*

From Deep Ecologists to Alchemists

Let's take this even one more step, to a very important concept. *We as magical people and Earth Healers are the rightful inheritors of the ancient art of alchemy.* The word *Alchemy* can mean many things, traditionally, historically, and magically. Historically alchemy had to do with those early Magicians who sought to transform and to *transmute* lead and other base metals into gold. I would like to suggest that we should strive for the ultimate form of magic, the *alchemy of the spirit.* The Gaia Group (GG) Book of Shadows teaches: "The Highest Magic is the Alchemy of the Spirit." Earlier we discussed the concept of "the Great Work." It too is an idea brought down to modern day from the alchemists of the Middle Ages and the Renaissance, the idea of always pursuing that which will lead to our highest spiritual development. In essence this phrase from the GG Book of Shadows refers to our vision of the Great Work.

It is common to become so demoralized by the environmental (and social) ills all around us that we become paralyzed and rendered mute. Or we become apathetic and demotivated. Since we are psychics and empaths who are in tune with Nature, we can very easily share the ail-ments, mentally and physically, besetting Mother Earth. The American medical and scientific professions have begun to realize the increasing numbers of illnesses that may be proliferating because of environmen-tal degradation of many kinds. The relatively new area of Western psy-chology known as "ecopsychology" studies this very phenomenon, seek-ing to redefine sanity and health within the context of humanity's very relationship to nature. However, this is where our spiritual power, faith, and commitment must assert itself. We who wish to heal the great Mother Gaia must take our rage and grief and sense of helplessness and *transmute* them into the most potent healing magic. We must protect ourselves and our loved ones magically while working our healing for the earth.

As we have seen, the good we do comes back to us in threes, through the magical Boomerang Effect. This becomes a kind of self-serving "bonus" for engaging in healing: receiving the marvelous loop it can create. (Although presumably, we really don't need any greater impetus for wishing to help our beleaguered planet than that alone.) Perhaps the highest possible act of alchemy is that *as we heal the Earth, we will also heal ourselves.* This is but one more reference to the miraculous cycles of interconnected cosmic energy.

But how should one go about achieving these wonderful, high-minded goals of healing the earth and oneself? Through the various Gaia Goals and other suggested activities, I have advocated two courses of action: working on the magical or metaphysical level *and* the mundane level—working on the astral plane *and* the physical plane.

To tie these ideas together with the three magical concepts discussed above, all of these adaptations in one's life go back to the point of magical hygiene. When you couple this kind of commitment on the physical level with consistent magical Earth Healing, you see the kind of power that can be built up. This power is added to constantly on the individual level and on the group level, which brings us again to connecting to the extended group mind.

I like to think of this philosophy as an "alchemy for the twenty-first century." The Craft priesthood and all people who honor and love the earth—whatever the moniker, background, philosophy, or tradition—have a responsibility. If we see ourselves as the inheritors of this magical pursuit of alchemy, then at what better time could we step forward than now, at the beginning of this new millennium? And in what better way could we possibly apply our magical arts on the highest level than by linking to Gaia's consciousness, working to heal the earth, and at the same time, healing ourselves. Truly this deserves the title of "Great Work."

Lunar Tides

One way to tap into this pool of energy is by paying attention to the tides of Nature, the forces that affect us and the natural world simultaneously. We are in contact with those tides unconsciously quite often. As we develop greater mindfulness, working with the changes of the moon can be a way of flowing with other natural forces around us.

Women are frequently in tune with these energies, since our bodies "wax and wane" like the moon through menstruation and ovulation. However, gardeners and farmers have from antiquity paid close attention to the phases of the moon in order to plant at the best time for maximizing growth and fertility. Of course, the seas and other bodies of water very obviously fall under the influence of the moon, and we must remember that our bodies, regardless of gender, are two-thirds water. How could we not be likewise influenced?

In any case, those who are drawn to Nature and who feel Gaia's call undoubtedly also feel the call of the moon. Her evocative nighttime face offers a most visible symbol of Goddess energy in the skies, and to Wiccans, Pagans, and indigenous people, she has many names. Whatever your spiritual background, the spell cast by a clear moonlight night, on snow or on grass, on pavement or on ocean, wherever you may be, is a potent one.

If you are just beginning a practice of magic, always factor in the phase of the moon when you work a rite or spell. In the broadest sense, for positive workings—that is, magic or intentions to do with growth, healing, new plans, prosperity, increase, abundance, and so on—you want to work with the *waxing* moon, when it cycles from new to full. Anything to do with lessening, losing, banishing, wiping away, decreasing, and so on should happen during the *waning* moon, from full to new moon. Some see this as a negative phase, but that term has so many unpleasant implications that perhaps the sense of diminishing or banishing is better.

However you term it, doing magic in the waning moon requires quite a bit of magical preparation and experience. So, I recommend that beginners on this path of Earth Spirituality and magic stay with the waxing moon energy. It is easier in many ways.

Let us begin to apply some of the concepts we have been discussing.

Deeper Dedication to Spiritual Evolution

Although you may feel that you already have a commitment to Earth Healing and to spiritually based activism, formalizing your commitment is an important psychological tool. It is in itself a trigger to move your mind and whole consciousness into a more actualized everyday process of living your magic and your ethos. Awareness and mindfulness are an ongoing process—they do not happen overnight and stay with us permanently without attention. The Hindu word for spiritual practice is *sadhana*. In many of the world's major religions, Christian, Buddhist, Islam, for example, the faithful are encouraged to live their spiritual practice, their sadhana. Ram Dass writes of this in *Be Here Now:* "At first you will think of your sadhana as a limited part of your life. In time you will come to realize that everything you do is part of your sadhana."

In Zen Buddhism there is a story that I have loved for years, and that has become a part of my family's life. (Strangely enough, and as universal wisdom works, I did not learn it from the great philosopher Alan Watts's writings or tapes, whose work I enjoy enormously, nor from my studies in comparative theology, but from my very wise Sicilian American aunt.)

A student comes to the Zen master and says, "Master, I have been working very hard on my spiritual process, trying everything that can bring me closer to enlightenment. But I need to know how to grow more. What else can I do?"

The Master answers, "Eat your rice and wash your bowl."

The student is very surprised and says, "But Master, I have meditated for hours and fasted for weeks. I have sat alone in a cave for months. What more can I do to approach enlightenment faster?"

"Eat your rice and wash your bowl."

And so it goes on. To each increasingly difficult act of sacrifice and personal spiritual commitment the student brings up, the Master replies the same: "Eat your rice and wash your bowl."

The moral of the story is that enlightenment and spiritual growth, the greatest pursuit of our sadhana, comes in small everyday ways—it is *how* we eat our rice and wash our bowl that matters. We bring the sacred with us each day, in all we do. As Jesus taught, the Kingdom of Heaven is within. Consequently, as we make formal acknowledgment of our sacred pursuit to be Deep Ecologists and Earth Healers, we grow in the smallest, mundane, and everyday acts. Our kitchen composting does indeed become an act of alchemy, as do all our acts. Baking bread by hand, not in a bread machine—with organic flour, of course!—kneading it, letting it rise, baking it . . . that must be one of the most alchemical, magical acts. I have often baked bread especially for rituals, with herbs and intentions added for specific purposes.

Now we will act out a rite of Self-Dedication to send that energy and resonance to all the planes of existence. This rite is a very simple one for those who wish to begin to make a commitment to both Gaia and to the path of magical Earth Healing in a more formalized fashion. Please perform this rite when the moon is waxing—when it is between the new moon and the full moon.

Exercise 24: Dedication to the Path of Gaian Magic

Center yourself and prepare to enact a very significant ritual. If you have a robe or some other special attire for ceremony, put it on. Or if you prefer to work skyclad, without clothing, then do so. Turn off the telephones and be sure that you will be undisturbed.

You will need a black cord to wear around your waist as a symbol of your Dedication. It should be 9 feet long.

Before your Dedication, you may want to choose a new name to use within the magic Circle and for other rituals. This is traditional in Wicca, as it is in other religions. It symbolizes the new person you are becoming, and can be a name that gives you inspiration or a role model to follow. Many Wiccans choose God and Goddess names, for example.

If you are already working ritual in a traditional Wiccan way, then you will want to have the Pentacle on the altar. If you do not have a Pentacle, then use a dish of earth, previously consecrated.

You may adapt the oath to add a dedication to the religion and Craft of Wicca, if that is your intention as well.

Center yourself and open your chakras. Perform the Self-Blessing, given in exercise 15. If you wish to construct the full Wiccan Circle, and do not already know how to do it, please see appendix B. Or you may set up sacred space in the way that feels right to you.

The Oath of Dedication

I, (here use your new magical name), standing in the Sacred Circle before the God, the Goddess, and the Elementals do swear without reservation:

That I have entered into magical training on the path of Earth Healing with sincerity and truth in my heart and with a clear desire to serve our Mother, this planet, and all of her children.

I further swear that I will follow the highest and most ethical path of magic, always intending to harm none in my spellcraft.

I swear that I will work with love and faith to learn that which I must learn.

I vow to bind myself to the Path of this Great Work, of divinely aided and inspired activism and Deep Ecology. Thus do I come with open heart to the religion of our Mother Earth.

Having sworn before the Gods and my brethren with my hand upon the Pentacle of Truth (or upon this symbol of Earth), I receive upon my head the Crown of New Beginnings.

Walk to each of the Four Quarters, the four directions, beginning in the East, and moving deosil, or clockwise. There, introduce yourself as a new Dedicant on the path of Earth Healing. You may say something like the following.

Beings of air, dwellers in the east, take note and duly heed that I, (your magical name), am a newly made Dedicant on the path of Earth Healing. Please guide me and teach me the gifts of air (or fire or water or earth.)

When you have finished with the Oath and with presenting yourself to the Quarters, consecrate your new cords for wearing whenever you do a Circle. They are the symbol of your commitment to magic and to your new spiritual path. Pass them carefully over the incense burner and the candles; also touch the consecrated water to the cords. Ask the Deity you have chosen to call into the Circle to aid you and bless you on your new path. You may also simply call upon the Great Spirit, or the Divine Spirit in a general way, maybe saying "Great Goddess and Great God." By passing the cords through the incense and over the candles and touching them with the salt and water, you are blessing and consecrating them not only in the names of the Divinity, but also through the aid of the Elementals, through those representative elements on the altar. When you have finished, you may close the Circle in the traditional Wiccan way, or you may close it in your tradition's style of working.

Remember to close your chakras down again afterward.

Having attested to this Oath, you have now become dedicated to the Old Gods and to the path of Gaian Earth Stewardship and Healing. If you are intending this as a first step on your Wiccan spiritual journey, this is the Neophyte Grade. Remember that this oath is a solemn act, and one that must not be taken lightly. You might like to copy the oath as written above, then sign and date it. You may sign with your new magical name or your own given name. Writing something down, or signing your name, makes an even greater psychological and spiritual impact, causing it to resonate that much more deeply for you.

Some years ago one of my students, a Temple of Gaia Priestess, Anya, was moved to write a special piece for her Dedication ceremony, which fell just before the Winter Solstice. It is such a beautiful, heartfelt poem that I asked her permission to include it for anyone who might like to use it or who might be inspired by it.

Dedication

I dedicate myself,
On this glorious winter night,
To the ways of Gaian Wicca,
And to healing, love, and light.

For I am a daughter to the Moon,
A sister to the Sea,
Fire is my father,
And the Wind is a lover to me.

The Earth is my grandmother,
She raised me with the trees,
Nature has been my home,
And dearest family.

I have heard the Goddess calling,
And seen Her at the door,
I have learned so much already,
And She wants to teach me more.

I wish to learn the mysteries,
And the ancient rites,
The secrets of the Mighty Ones,
And the language of moonlight.

I dedicate myself to training,
My body, soul, and mind,
To become a Wiccan Priestess,
And to leave what's old behind.

So I ask upon the heavens,
To the great Diana and to Lugh,
Take me as a Neophyte,
And teach me what is true.

Blessed Be.

It is very fulfilling to write your own words for ceremony. However, it may take some practice and time, especially if you are not already inclined to writing. Many of the books in the reading list offer pieces that can be memorized and used for ritual, meditation, prayer, or spellcraft. Some spells are traditional, as are other pieces like the Charge of the Goddess, and are used all over the world in the same form. This gives them a particular power of their own. However, you can take some pieces or rituals and adapt them for your own use. (I personally believe in always giving credit to my sources, even if a piece is simply used in a ritual for my coven.)

We spoke earlier of work that raises one's vibration. The kind of personal commitment expressed by a Self-Dedication, in the presence of the Gods and the Mighty Ones within the magic Circle, is a very weighty act that accelerates one's personal spiritual evolution. We your human brethren and all your nonhuman brethren salute you and your commitment to helping the earth. Congratulations on having the courage to make such a leap. And welcome brothers and sisters in Gaia!

Other Rituals and Magic for Specific Causes

Just as it is appropriate to work magic with the Elementals of the land you live in, in Paganism and in Wicca it is appropriate to work magic with Gods or Goddesses of the Pantheon who most relate to the magic you are doing. It is also advisable to choose those who relate best to the time of year and the cause you are working for.

For instance, if you plan to do a piece of magic in a ritual about saving forests in North America, call upon the help of Deities who are connected with forests and, if you are so inclined, those connected with North America. From the Native American tradition, you could call upon the Corn Maiden, Grandmother Spider, White Buffalo Calf

Woman, or so many others. If you are in the Southwestern United States, you might resonate to the Mexican Earth Mother Goddess, Tonantzin, called by the Spanish and much loved by today's Mexican people as the Lady of Guadalupe. Some Old World Gods who many Wiccans resonate to are Cernunnos, Lord of the Forest; Pan, God of Nature and the Animal Kingdom; Diana, Lady of the Hunt and the Forests; Isis and Osiris, connected with the River Nile and with vegetation, as well as with healing and magic.

My tradition tends to work with Old World Deities—European, Egyptian, Hindu, and even African—rather than North American or Native American. However, as I have mentioned, I do call upon the Elemental rulers of this land for aid in all I do. (Personally I also often call on the Latin American Elementals and Goddesses because of time and studies spent in this area.)

Spellcraft and magical technique, like so many of the magical practices we have discussed in this book, take months and years of practice to learn. Taking each exercise in this book step by step will help you to develop the power of visualization and the intense concentration you need, while maintaining a split-focus or dual-consciousness in magic making. We must retrain our modern minds to learn ancient practices and recapture dormant abilities in the ancient, nonlinear parts of our brains. With these exercises you are well on the way to recapturing these powerful skills known to our ancestors.

Here are just a few examples of the kinds of rituals and actions that various Wiccan groups, including my own Gaia Group, have taken to help heal the earth. Some of these might sound preposterous or full of hubris, but I honestly believe that we have influenced some large environmental concerns in recent years.

On Earth Day some years ago, Myrddin, Crystal, and I decided to take on legislation being designed by the U.S. Congress that would dismantle various environmental protections that we had all worked desperately to achieve over the previous thirty years. Due to the constraints and concerns of karma, we do not try to impact people directly, but we aim our magical powers at legislation, policies, campaigns, and so on. Although I could use more "karmically challenging" spells, I have always been careful with anything aimed at stopping people or legislation. Usually my technique is to stop things "cold" shall I say. . . . There is a magical technique called freezing that halts actions in their tracks. In the months after our ritual, certain well-known bills failed and disappeared, and certain legislators' powers seemed to wane considerably.

Again without using too many specifics (to protect ourselves and other people involved), the Temple of Gaia group decided to take action against a particularly egregious act of environmental destruction being carried out in a rural area largely inhabited by Hispanic farmers. A wealthy outside interest was destroying the area's forests, watershed, and lands, thereby jeopardizing the local people's livelihoods. In a ritual, the Temple of Gaia created a thoughtform (this technique creates an astral entity by means of magical visualization and will who then acts as the agent for the task at hand) to stop the logging, a kind of gentle green giant of the forest. (Remember Treebeard in Tolkien's masterpiece, *The Lord of the Rings*? Something like him, in my mind.)

A Pagan friend and regional environmentalist who was involved in the protests held in this rural area told the local residents about our magical assistance. Being of Mexican descent, the people loved the idea and took it very much to heart. They claimed that they *saw* our friendly giant helper/thoughtform, in fact, walking about the forests, and it helped them by fueling their own commitment and activism.

Some years ago we performed a ritual with a more distant focus: to stop nuclear testing in the Pacific. A European government was carrying out a series of nuclear tests on small islands, or atolls, in the South Pacific. The bombs were huge, many times the size of those dropped in Hiroshima and Nagasaki, and were causing devastating effects on the sea life, the atolls, and the people in the region. We asked for the aid of Athena and Poseidon (Athena is the Goddess of wisdom, government, and war; Poseidon is the God of the Sea; both are from the Greek pantheon) to change the minds of the foreign government's leaders and to stop the testing. We did not direct any hostility toward the government involved, of course. We simply sent the leaders "thoughts of peace, wisdom, and a realization of what they are doing so they will stop" (in the words of the Priestess who wrote the ritual).

We performed a standard Circle, in our GG/Temple of Gaia style, but evoking Athena and Poseidon instead of the Deities we normally invite into the Circle. In an example of talismanic magic, we had made tinfoil models of nuclear missiles, which we dismantled and tore up. While doing that, we clearly visualized the testing ending and the government dismantling their nuclear missiles.

Through my international contacts, I learned that a coven on the other side of the world (South Africa) did a similar ritual near the same time. Undoubtedly their magical activism coupled with our own (perhaps also with others I don't know of) had an influence on the nuclear testing program in the atoll. Six months after our ritual, the testing was stopped, the test site was dismantled, and all future testing was changed to computer simulations.

One of the traditional tenets of magic is that it is best to rhyme your spells. This is because the unconscious and deeper levels of the mind, sometimes called our inner child, respond well to the sound and rhythm of the rhymes. Rhymes also are much easier to remember—particularly if you are teaching the spell to the coven for the first time on the night of the ritual. When as an actress I learned long Shakespearean pieces or other kinds of monologues, it was always easier to remember them if the pieces were in verse. Keep your spells short and to the point, and make them rhyme.

Here's an example from the South Pacific ritual above:

No more bombs,
No more radiation!
No more destruction or devastation!
The _____ will change,
They will put their bombs away;
This is our will and for this we pray!

It is also best if the rhythm is a bit "catchy" and easy to move to. Another of the traditional teachings about magical spells is that it is good to *dance* them, that is, to move around the circle, clockwise or "deosil," dancing and chanting. (Notice similarities to other Earth religions? All the world's people's unconscious minds work in similar fashions.) We visualize as we dance, keeping the mental image of what we hope to achieve. Therefore it is much, much easier to say the words while visualizing if the spell and chant are short and very rhythmic.

I have not saved many of our spells in written form, unlike invocations or other parts of the ritual. (Perhaps because we often compose them spontaneously right before we perform the magical act and I do not write them down.) However, here are two more examples from spells we used and added to our Book of Shadows, though not from our Earth Healing magic.

The first I saved is a fertility spell, created by former Temple of Gaia member Mannanan. It was written to help a couple conceive a child:

Join the body and the soul
Take the two and make them whole.
Plant the seed and make the child,
In a night of passion wild.

As I mentioned earlier, Paganism and Wicca smile upon and encourage the sensual pleasures, particularly when shared between committed partners in a stable relationship. For example, sex magic is a very ancient and very powerful area of magical training, used not only for conception but also for any magical intent. This is another area of crossover between Hinduism and Wicca; there are quite a few techniques of sex magic that may have come directly from Tantra, an ancient Hindu school of training. The spell given above was not used in a sex magic ritual by the coven, it was simply danced as a way of sending fertility energy to the couple hoping for a child.

The second example of a simple spell in rhyme comes from our Autumn Equinox ritual. The GG and the Temple of Gaia have a tradition of blessing nonperishable food to donate to the community Food Bank as the cold months draw on. I love this custom and the idea that the recipients receive much more than just the physical cans and boxes:

Strength and health and hope we give
That a sweeter life soon you'll live!

I shared this idea with a local church and they have adopted a style of the technique. Each month the food collected at the church for donation to the local Food Bank is "blessed" or charged with prosperity energy by the whole congregation, a kind of group laying on of hands. The congregation has entitled that particular Sunday "Compassionate Sunday." It is a beautiful and powerful community visualization that can have a huge impact on all planes—a perfect example of working on both the sacred and the mundane levels.

Once Burned, Twice Shy

My coven has also had some near disasters—even doing magic alone, I have occasionally caused results I did not count on. I am not ashamed to admit these outcomes and will share some stories to aid others in avoiding such pitfalls. Being Nature Magicians and people intimately in tune with the forces of Nature means that we must very carefully evaluate the possible outcomes of our actions in magic. Even with the best and most admirable of intentions, we can unleash forces so extraordinarily powerful that we can cause havoc.

Again, this may sound like arrogance or hubris. However, I am speaking from direct personal experience to warn those venturing into new magical territories. The experience I'll relate has humbled me in the face of knowing what awe-inspiring powers await our call, just at the edge of human consciousness. Like medieval alchemists who experimented with metals and chemicals in pursuit of transmuting lead or other elements into gold and instead triggered explosions they never expected, we modern Magicians and Alchemists can set off reactions in the Elements, too.

One particularly clear example is in the area of weather magic. One might think that for a Witch or Pagan, weather magic should be the first and simplest magic to attempt. As even the medieval Inquisitors were quick to mention, Witches were legendary for their power to influence and control the weather. However, it is *not simple,* and it can be extremely dangerous. Perhaps it is due to the fact that Mother Gaia is wounded and not well at this time in her evolution, or because the Elementals have been out of close touch with humanity for some centuries. Whatever the exact reason, I will warn prospective weather and Nature Magicians to proceed with enormous caution.

One year when Colorado was facing a huge drought, my coven and I decided to ask for some rain to end the drought. Well, it began to rain. And rain. And rain. Soon the area was confronted with what might become the "hundred year flood"—whole parts of the city's downtown could have been wiped out. The city's administrators prepared for the potential flood with evacuation procedures, siren warnings, stockpiled sandbags, and so on. Finally, after much anxiety, the hundred year flood did not happen that year . . . thankfully. And the Temple of Gaia learned an essential lesson.

The next most impressive lesson came a few years later with a different set of Initiates. We had grown very concerned about the pace of development in this area of Colorado and decided to do an act of Earth Healing to stop some of it. The idea was to cleanse Colorado of people's greed and materialistic view of the earth. Later, one Priestess told me that she had visualized a huge broom sweeping the greed and rampant development away. This may have had some connection to the result of our magic.

In traditional magic, the teaching says that the results of spells may take weeks or even months. In weather and Nature magic, it can take hours or only minutes, judging by the results I have seen.

The day after our cleansing ritual, the sky turned an unheard-of color at noontime—a sickening shade of yellow. By midafternoon sirens sounded across the city, and something almost never imagined had happened: a tornado had touched down in this county. Tornadoes happen fairly regularly on the plains of eastern Colorado, but never close to the mountains. This so-called freak occurrence reached within four miles of the foothills.

I have other similarly strange and unbelievable stories of such occurrences after acts of weather or Nature magic. All I can say is that one must be exceptionally careful with the powerful forces that are waiting nearby for our partnership. This is true in all magic, but the extraordinary immediacy of Nature magic shows the potential dangers. In my opinion it is particularly true when one is dedicated to and adept at working with the Elementals, through building the close working relationship we discussed in chapter 4.

I should add that since these undesired outcomes, I have learned a few things. The first is to be very clear on the purpose and the possible results. Prepare the ritual and the magic very carefully. The second is to always add a few lines to the spell asking that it result in the highest and best destiny for any and all involved.

In Closing

We have traveled a long way together in the course of this book. You have launched yourself well on the path of magical Earth Stewardship and enlightened activism. It may be "the road less traveled," but maybe through your fine examples that will not be the case forever! You will never walk into the woods or onto a seashore, stroll through a park or camp in Nature with the same eyes . . . you will forever see and connect with energies and beings that many do not acknowledge. Your concept of wildlife and wilderness will have changed as well. Your heart will be reenchanted by Gaia, and as you fall in love with life again, you will feel renewed. Remember that this awareness and this communion is a gift, but it also brings a responsibility. You can now truly be an agent for change and a midwife to the birth of new consciousness across the planet. You are indeed an integral part of Gaia's consciousness.

Gaia Goals

If composting is an alchemical act, and water is a magic elixir of life, and crystals carry ancient messages, what more truly practical magic can we incorporate in our daily lives?

- Start a compost pile or bin in your yard, in the communal garden nearby, or with friend in his or her garden. It will bring a guaranteed thrill when you first see the richly fertile, dark soil your kitchen alchemy has helped create.

- Remember the interdependent web of life—another magical metaphor, similar to the web of magic that connects the cosmos. We are all connected—live it, eat low on it, protect it.

- "Raise a ruckus," as one of my most daring environmentalist friends says—make our leaders hear your voice. Mount campaigns for what is needed in your community for the environment, for wildlife, for humane and conscious living.

- Keep the macro picture that being in communion with Gaia brings, and fight the NIMBY mentality, "Not in My Backyard." Toxic waste, pollution, pesticides, nuclear power, overfishing, logging unsustainably anywhere hurts Gaia and us all.

- Volunteer your time and donate anything you can—money, food, clothing, bedding—to local shelters for battered women or the homeless, to soup kitchens, to centers for emergency family assistance. And while you are there, send a blessing and some protective energy. Infuse the food or goods you donate, consecrate them with magic healing. Make your magical activism a constant way of life!

Epilogue

No, wilderness is not a luxury but a necessity of the human
spirit, and as vital to our lives as water and good bread.
A civilization which destroys what little remains of the wild,
the spare, the original, is cutting itself off from its origins and
betraying the principle of civilization itself.

Edward Abbey

Edward Abbey, the great writer and environmentalist supreme, also
wrote that the love of wilderness is "an expression of loyalty to the earth,
the earth which bore us and sustains us, the only home we shall ever
know, the only paradise we ever need...." One could easily substitute the
word *Nature* for *wilderness* in the passages quoted from Abbey. Nature
is not a luxury; it is a staff of our lives.

It is my hope that this book will have inspired you to recognize and
to express your loyalty to Mother Gaia by bringing more Earth Healing
practices into your life. Whether you are a longtime environmentalist, a
Wiccan of many years' experience, or a person just venturing onto this
path, these ancient healing practices and techniques will aid you in bringing love and rebirth into the world. At the same time they will aid you
in healing your own despair or disillusionment as you deepen your communion with the earth.

Tragically, the old paradigms of the earth-destroying and earth-
consuming patriarchies still hold sway over our Western societies.
Despite the birth of the Age of Aquarius and the reborn environmental
consciousness taking hold in pockets around the world, the old orders
fight to maintain their dominion.

As I wrote this closing in its initial draft, a magnificent document,
"The Earth Charter," was being presented to the world (you can view the
text of the charter online at www.earthcharterusa.org or contact Earth
Charter USA Campaign, 2100 L Street, NW, Washington, DC 20037, tel:
202-778-6133; fax: 202-778-6138). It proposes a world of peaceful and
sustainable society, of living in harmony and respect with each other and
the earth, through the development of truly democratic, environmentally sound communities. A gathering of 300 people in the Netherlands
on June 29, 2000, watched at the Peace Palace as the Earth Charter was
presented to Queen Beatrix. The goal of the next phase of development

is to gather international political and religious support for endorsement of the Earth Charter by the United Nations in 2002. However, despite support by such world leaders as former Premier Mikhail Gorbachev, the Honorable Maurice Strong, Professor Steven Rockefeller, and former Vice President Al Gore, this life-honoring document came under strident attack from the Vatican and some other religious organizations of the Muslim and Christian world. Why? Because it honors the earth and therefore was called "pagan" and seen as evil.

This is doubly ironic, as no Pagans were involved in its creation. In fact, Pagans have no official presence in the United Nations, even though Paganism represents many ancient and modern world religions. Paganism and the Earth Charter, in the eyes of conservative, fundamentalist organizations, are equated with the "work of the devil." It is always shocking to realize that such attitudes endure, remarkably similar to those of the infamous medieval and Renaissance leaders of the Inquisition. Therefore the Vatican and other fundamentalist groups urged their followers to oppose this philanthropic document that promotes sustainable living for all the earth's peoples.

I mention the Earth Charter and this event as an example of the need for greater spiritual activism and mundane-plane activism. It is time for all who hear Gaia's voice to come out of our hiding places, out of our TV and computer rooms, out of our cars and SUVs, out of our secure little bubbles. For those who are Witches and Wiccans, step out of the broomcloset at last. We must be both witnesses and evidence to the birth of a new paradigm of harmonious, environmentally conscious thought.

Remember that as you become more and more connected to the web of life, to the web of energy all around us, your compassion for all life will grow. And as your compassion grows, so will your wisdom and your personal spiritual power. Therefore, you will be an activist for greater compassion in the world, spreading the message of this new paradigm through your magical work and your everyday life. Remember the "drive-by blessings" we talked about in chapter 2—you can also become quiet perpetrators of anonymous blessings wherever you go, if you wish.

Let your devotion to the Divine force in Nature, to the Great Spirit, to the Gods, the Elementals, and the realms of Nature sustain this journey. Let your loyalty to the earth also sustain you. When you feel truly committed to this path and have begun your training in earnest, and perhaps have performed the Oath of Dedication, tell others. Pray, meditate,

do magic—*and* write letters, make phone calls, go to peaceful demon-
strations, and participate in Direct Actions. Make your voice heard, on
this plane and on others! As an activist, you must take an active role on
all planes. Talk about it with people whose hearts seem open to hearing
Gaia.

It is so easy to become complacent, to assume we can let others pick
up the standard. It is also terribly easy to hit the wall emotionally and
encounter psychic "burnout." Yet we must aim to first heal ourselves,
since our work is that of a healer. Refresh your perspectives (and your
chi) by getting out in Nature and having some fun! Laugh, play, splash
in creeks or the ocean, roll in fresh grass or fallen leaves; sit with a loved
one and watch the stars. Remember how you loved all that as a child.
Allow yourself to be re-enchanted. As you allow Gaia's enchantments to
seduce you and charm you, as her potent energies flow through you, you
will overcome disillusionment, fatigue, cynicism, or indifference. A most
miraculous transmutation will take place within you. And you will
become a true magical activist and Alchemist for the twenty-first century.

Let Gaia speak to you more and more. Remember you are part of
her very awareness; you are an extension of her. You will hear her call
and the call of our brethren on this planet—those with voices like our
own and those with other means of communicating. In doing so, your
work will sustain us all, now and in time to come.

Pro Terra cum Amore et Animo ("For the earth with love and
courage"—motto of the Temple of Gaia).

Blessed Be!

Appendix A[6]

A List of Crystal Helpers

The following names and applications of some favorite "helpers" are listed in order of their relation to the chakras, crown to base. This is not intended to be a comprehensive list of all healing or magic-related crystals.

Crown Chakra—Clear, white, opalescent colors

Clear Quartz—Energizes, transmits, balances, heals, protects. The basic, all-encompassing, all-purpose stone. Clear quartz can be used to "tap in to" all color frequencies. Excellent for charging water to make an all-purpose crystal "elixir."

White Diamond—Clarifies, focuses, gives a "hard edge" to intellectual or cerebral processes; must be used with care, however, because like all white stones, white diamonds can be easily programmed and are very powerful amplifiers.

Herkimer Diamond—Brightens, lightens, clarifies. A stone formed in water, therefore light, bubbly, floating feminine energy.

Pearl—Not a crystal, but it has a very changeable, soft, feminine, lunar energy; pearls can be used for their great "emotional absorbency." Like crystals, these take on the wearer's attributes. However, they do not harmonize in the same way.

Opal—Potent psychic power aids; very changeable and absorbent—use with care! Some say only those whose birthstone is opal should use them, but I believe that those willing to experience both the Dark and the Light may experience their power. (Some books place opal at the heart chakra because of their influence on the emotions and help in balancing them.)

Moonstone—This stone is very connected to feminine energies, particularly those to do with balancing the sexual organs, with fertility, and with aiding in pregnancy, childbirth, and child-rearing. Some call it the "Mother Earth" stone, but as its name implies, it is governed directly by the moon. The color varies greatly—it can be opalescent, an iridescent silvery gray with a lunar light in its depths, yellow to peach to dark gray. As this stone can vary in color, so its uses vary with the color.

Third Eye Chakra—Violet, indigo

Amethyst—Uplifts and greatly stimulates the intuition and psychic and spiritual natures; a gentle but powerful healer and transmitter. It is the greatest "eye-opener" for the third eye, opening the so-called Divine Channel—crown to third eye. It is probably the best starter for beginning crystal workings.

Fluorite—A supremely magical transmitter, receiver, and balancer; said by some to have been brought to Earth from the Pleiades for the highest level of spiritual and psychic development. Most people familiar with it cannot emphasize its Divine powers enough—three tones symbolize well its role of connecting the divine with the human spirit and the physical plane.

Lapis Lazuli—"The Witch's Stone"; heightens psychic insight, clarifying intuition and vision while calming and protecting against psychic attack or intrusion. A great wisdom and power enhancer, it is revered by many evolved ancient cultures, especially those that honored their Priests, Priestesses, Seers, Mystics, and Visionaries.

Sodalite—A cleanser and balancer; lowers blood pressure while aiding metabolism. It has a gently empowering effect emotionally, instilling confidence and courage. (Makes an excellent elixir for cleansing and balancing the endocrine system.)

Sapphire—One of the "princes" of stones; revered for centuries for its power and beauty; considered to be the stone of destiny, truth, and idealism. Like all multicolored stones—see Addendum—it taps in to different energy frequencies depending on the shade, but generally the sapphire is related to hope and faith, as well as being a gentle tranquilizer.

Throat Chakra—Aqua, light blue, turquoise

Aquamarine—A powerful communication enhancer and problem-solving tool; it brings good humor to the wearer (which can easily be projected through its use to those near). It aids in opening the energy channel to spirit-mind-body flow for releasing negativity and finding answers to problems and blocks. (But can be very uncomfortable to those with fifth-chakra blockages!)

Turquoise—A power strengthener and an aid to confidence; sacred to the Native Americans as the truest embodiment of the spiritual connection between humanity and the natural world. A gentle but effective healer and protector—but soft and porous, so it must be worn or used carefully. Also seen as "lucky."

Blue Topaz—A gentle stress reliever and calmer; like aquamarine, a communication enhancer, but much more delicate in easing blocks. (Less "explosive" than its yellow and brown shades.)

Heart Chakra—Greens, dark and light; also pink

Peridot—The "get and up and go" stone; it helps to motivate by clearing and cleansing the organs and toxins. It is considered an overall tonic for body and mind that accelerates personal growth and helps to overcome lethargy, laziness, and procrastination. It also clears old emotional blockages and heals old lingering wounds impeding growth.

Chrysophrase—A subtle joy stone that calms and balances, healing throughout the emotional body. Said to bring out inner talents and enhance personal insight, while bestowing a sense of lightheartedness. Especially potent for Pisceans.

Moldavite—Considered an extra-terrestrial stone, this is said to come from a meteorite that landed on certain parts of Earth some 15 million years ago. It endows the user with celestial psychic healing and visionary capacities, as well as functioning as a general tonic and personal balancer. Powerful in the extreme for some. (Also said to be powerful in communicating psychically with other forms of intelligence, such as dolphins and whales!)

Emerald—The stone and frequency of love (Venus); it can aid in developing both clarity of vision regarding love affairs and is literally good for the eyesight! It has a calming, soothing effect overall and helps the heart center to expand gently with unconditional love.

Rose Quartz—The gentle peace bringer and healer of emotional wounds; it has a gladdening, uplifting effect that makes one more open to others and promotes kindness and friendship. A good, all-purpose heart-flow opener and healer—less abrupt and sudden than Kunzite.

Watermelon Tourmaline—The chameleon of stones—a gentle male/female energy balancer, good for healing emotional wounds and for moving on to new life phases. It lifts the spirits to cheery goodwill while instilling peace, cooperation, and for-giveness. Will not absorb negativity. Comes in pink-green com-binations, as well as blue and black. (See addendum regarding multicolored stones.)

Malachite—A gentle peace bringer that energizes softly with a sense of security and confidence; it protects and strengthens the heart and helps to balance prosperity energy as it instills self-confidence. It aids in keeping the spirit-mind-body flow open by dispelling illusions. Be warned: like opal, it may break if dan-ger, excessive negativity, or disaster is imminent.

Kunzite—Explodes heart center blockages; cleanses and washes out anger, self-hate, inability to love. Use when more powerful heart-expanding and purging is needed than crystal quartz—but only when prepared for effects. Good for balancing femi-nine energies by giving a strong dose of yin/Venus energy. Can be purple pink or green.

Solar Plexus Chakra—Yellow and gold

Yellow Citrine—Centers, roots, balances, integrates head and body energies, and aids creativity; the effective but smooth paver of the clear path between spiritual, mental, and visceral (Earth) energies. It helps to solve disputes internally and to evolve disci-pline regarding wants and moral/ethical issues. Also eases toxins out of the system.

Topaz—Powerful sun energy—very solar/male. Though extremely energizing to the solar center, it centers mind/body energy flow and so helps to balance the nervous and circulatory system.

Tiger's Eye—A stone of evolution—solidifying, steadying, protect-ing. Often considered a prized amulet of good luck and psychic shielding by ancient cultures, it aids intuitive/visionary develop-ment while balancing and steadying. Multiple color variations bring in many color frequency vibrations—down through the legs to Earth and up to the Astral through silvery gray.

Yellow Calcite— Gently expands the solar center, integrating ener-gies, raising spirits, helping intuitive powers; a gentler, more joyful, less cerebral discernment/judgment aid than citrine, but similar in balancing effect.

Root Chakra—Orange and golden orange to nearly red

Carnelian—Called the "Valium of the Astral" (a tranquilizer); it grounds you to the earth and helps to calm nerves, tension, flightiness. Mental focus is affected gently but effectively. It helps with intestinal imbalances by stimulating the adrenals, aiding digestion and absorption of nutrients. When applied to the lower chakras can also be balancing to sexual glands and energies.

Orange Citrine—See yellow citrine, above, and the addendum regarding multicolored stones.

Amber—Not a crystal—it is actually fossilized tree resin—but still a powerful tool. A negativity absorber and polarity balancer; long revered for amulets, magical workings, and healing potential. It also has a gentle male/female centering effect. Can help to break emotional/sexual blockages and to relax sexual rigidity. The color can vary from light yellow to deep red.

Base Chakra—Deep reds and blacks; deepest hues

Ruby—A mood elevator and an enhancer of courage and intuition. The ruby has been cherished and revered as the most deeply "charged" with ancient knowledge on the spiritual plane. It connects to God/Goddess energy most powerfully as manifested through Love, and therefore is a heart/spirit/sexuality energizer.

Hematite—Also called "silverstone" or "bloodstone"; a greatly revered African power stone; ground up it becomes a red face or body paint used by tribes to strengthen blood and symbolize courage and power. It opens the energy pathways to the earth.

Smoky Quartz—Has a wonderful balancing effect on the energy from crown to base; it helps those not well connected with the earth plane to connect in a healthy, loving manner. Helps those with the highest ideals to manifest dreams and goals on Earth.

Obsidian—Called the "dynamite of the Astral," it can be used to explode blocks of all kinds and to expel negativity, but one must be prepared for the results. Its shiny surface is often used for scrying or divining and for its ability to connect the user with the unconscious. Should be used with great care and prior understanding.

Dark stones, black and gray, can generally be used for their settling, absorbing, very heavy Earth energy connecting powers. They relate to the legs and the pathways from the lower body down through the feet into the earth.

Addendum

Regarding Multicolored Stones

The fundamental potential and energy of stones does not change with their color variations. However, their energy center applications, relationships, and specific uses can change with the color "frequency" or the clarity. In other words, if the stones are to be used for healing, chakra, or magical work, one should choose the color that is related to the specific chakra for the desired energy result.

Quartz—Besides clear quartz and crystal quartz, there are many color variations including blue and black (not including the other related quartz family stones).

Diamond—Very rare, but can be yellow and pink.

Opal—White, blue, pink purple, all with multicolored fires; rarest are deep blue and black.

Moonstone—Milky gray white, silvery opalescent, peach, heavy gray.

Fluorite—White/clear, purple, green.

Sapphire—Blue, pink, green, yellow.

Tourmaline—Blue, green, watermelon pink, black.

Citrine—Yellow, orange, dusky yellow brown.

Topaz—Yellow, light blue, deep aqua.

Calcite—White, yellow, green.

Carnelian—Yellow orange, deep orange, muddy brick red.

Amber—Pale to deep yellow orange, orange, brick red.

Obsidian—Black to blackish brown to gray black spotted with gray.

Agate—Moss (white and green), brown, yellow, crystal, multicolored.

Garnet—Bright ruby-red, deep wine, or dark to black.

Appendix B

The Wiccan Circle Casting

Many readers may feel that they have progressed to a point in their training as magical Deep Ecologists and Earth Magicians where it is appropriate to learn to create a fully protected magical Circle in a traditional Wiccan style. Others may not be interested, and may not feel it necessary for their spiritual activism. Follow your heart—you can be an effective spiritual activist for Gaia without being Wiccan, of course! I did not intend this book only for Wiccans or Pagans. However, if you are interested in learning a method of Wiccan Circle casting, I offer it here.

If you are already using another form of Circle casting, or creating some other tradition's sacred space, continue to construct sacred space as you feel most comfortable. If you do not know how to build the magic Circle Wiccan style, I will teach you the form used in my tradition.

Because Wicca is a living, growing religion, the method of Circle Casting can vary from Circle to Circle. This is how new Initiates in the Temple of Gaia learn the Circle, so that all have a consistent practice to work together and to grow from. If you are new to this path or this tradition, it is best to memorize the full Circle Casting word for word. The better you knows the words, the easier it is to visualize while speaking. In working with a group, it is essential to have the words solidly "by heart."

Casting the Magic Circle

The ritual space should be clean and attractive—you will be inviting the Deities and Elementals, honored guests, to join here with you. And of course, the space must be free of distractions: no telephone, computer, TV, radio. Ritual music is wonderful and can be very helpful, if it is not distracting but rather consciousness-enhancing. Remember the "triggers" we discussed earlier—find the triggers that help you to shift consciousness to a ritual and magic mindframe. Certain music may do that for you. You are setting the scene to create the World Between the Worlds. We discussed earlier how sacred drama and the actor/shaman are the origins of theater. This is like a stage setting that calls for a magnificently magical scene, and every bit of the set or staging is important. However, you may keep it simple. The intention and the triggers to aid your concentration and shift of consciousness are most important.

If you have not yet acquired a ritual robe, either made specially by you, or chosen from among your wardrobe to be a ritual robe, you should do so. You may also work skyclad, without any clothing, if that is your tradition or if that feels right to you. Certainly if you do work robed, go barefoot and wear little or nothing beneath your robe. Clothing of any kind can impede and restrict your personal power. Significant jewelry is nice to wear, perhaps a crystal necklace that you have designated as your ritual jewelry, or a bracelet or ring. Many choose to wear jewelry with ancient symbols like a pentagram, an ankh, or a spiral. Your jewelry should also be consecrated in the Circle for ritual use. And a widely observed magical tenet is to never wear a watch or allow a clock in the Circle—it is the time outside of time.

The altar and, if desired, the Watchtowers at each quarter of the Circle are prepared in advance. For those new to the path of Wicca and Earth Spirituality, a simple altar will do: a pretty cloth perhaps with significant colors or designs, some sacred objects, perhaps some God or Goddess symbols or statues, flowers, candles, incense, and so on. You will need salt and water, in separate dishes to begin with, for the Circle Casting. Oil that has been consecrated or charged with a blessing is necessary too. The altar is usually placed in the north of the Circle. However, the altar can also be placed in the center of the Circle according to our tradition.

You may want to have a chalice of wine, ale, or simply juice, to make a "libation" or offering to the Gods during the Circle. You can also have cakes, cookies, or bread as an offering. If you wish to have some symbolic objects in each quarter of the Circle to represent each of the elements, that is appropriate and can be helpful for the visualizations at each quarter. (Crystals, stones, or dirt for earth; shells or a basin for water; and so on.) Or you can simply put a candle, in your tradition's colors for each quarter. If you are not sure what colors to use, think of what you identify with each element— (e.g., green for earth, white for air, red for fire, blue for water). In the beginning the most important practice is to learn to form a very solid visualization.

All should be properly prepared and purified prior to the Rite; for example the Self-Blessing given in exercise 15 is an appropriate way to begin. Upon entering the ritual area, all participants join hands and stand around the altar in meditation to open and align their chakras, or the participants may stand in the center in a Circle, holding hands. The focus should be to reinforce group harmony.

When the Circle casting is completed, and it is no longer necessary to hold hands, the Gaia Group/Temple of Gaia protocol is to stand in the

"God position," or the Osiris position, with arms crossed over the chest and hands resting on the opposite shoulders.

The High Priest (HP) or High Priestess (HPS), depending on the season, casts the Circle with one of the magical tools, a wand, Athame, or sword, East to East deosil (clockwise). From the spring equinox to the fall equinox, the HPS does the casting; then, from fall to spring, the coven sword returns to the HP. He or she draws energy through his or her body and projects it through the magical tool, creating an ovoid sphere of blue energy surrounding the entire ritual space. The Officiate recites outwardly or inwardly the following:

> **I conjure and command thee,**
> **O Magic Circle of Power,**
> **That thou be a faithful boundary and a refuge,**
> **Between the world of humans and the realms of the Mighty Ones,**
> **A stern guardian and steadfast protection**
> **That shall preserve and contain the power**
> **That we shall raise within thee.**
> **Wherefore art thou established**
> **In the names of _____ and _____.**

(Here insert the names of the Deities that you wish to call upon in the rite.)

> **So Mote It Be.**

(This expression, commonly used in Wicca and Paganism, means "So be it" or Amen. All usually join the Officiate in answering in unison.) With the wand or Athame, the HPS or HP officiating purifies the water, using the same technique as consecration, willing the water to be purified through magical energy. He or she says:

> **I exorcise thee O creature of water,**
> **That thou cast out from thee**
> **All impurities and uncleanliness**
> **In the names of _____ and _____. So Mote It Be.**

The salt is blessed on the Pentacle in a similar manner:

> **Blessings be upon thee, O creature of Earth.**
> **Let all malignity and hindrance be cast henceforth,**
> **And let all good enter herein.**
> **Wherefore do I bless thee**

In the names of _____ **and** _____.
So Mote It Be.

The officiate adds the salt to the water and says:

But ever let us be mindful,
That as water purifies the body,
So does salt purify the spirit.

The officiate censes the Circle, East to East, deosil. The officiate then asperges the Circle with the consecrated salt and water, East to East, deosil.

The officiate now erects the Watchtowers of the Circle, East to East, deosil. With the wand or Athame, the officiate begins at the eastern quarter, salutes the Lord of the Watchtower, then traces an invoking Pentagram of Earth (the upright Pentagram or Witches' Five-pointed Star), saying the following:

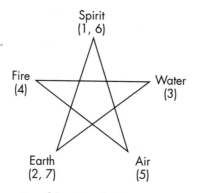

Invoking Earth Pentagram

Beings of air/fire/water/earth,
Dwellers in the East/South/West/North,
I do summon, stir and call ye up,
To witness our Rites and guard this Circle.
And I do bid ye, Hail and Welcome!
(All participants repeat: **Hail and Welcome!**)

If desired, a co-officiate or other Priest/Priestess may stand beside the officiate, holding the symbol of the element toward the Watchtower as the officiate says the above. After the Pentagram is traced, the officiate and all present salute the Watchtower, either by pointing their Athames or their right index and middle fingers. As the officiate finishes calling the Watchtower, he or she will kiss the Athame and point it again. Each participant may do likewise. Another tradition is to add a half-bow to each quarter. This is done while repeating: **"Hail and Welcome."**

The officiate will proceed to each cardinal point in turn, until he or she returns to the East point and again salutes.

The HPS anoints the HP and all members of the Circle with previously consecrated oil. The HP (or other male Priest, if there is no HP) then anoints the HPS. Some covens prefer to have the HPS anoint the male participants and the HP or acting HP anoint the females. This can be varied according to the coven's wishes and working practice. Our tradition is usually to do it as above, tracing an upward pointing Pentagram on the forehead of each participant with consecrated oil. This is done while speaking a blessing and welcoming each person into the Circle.

In the Temple of Gaia we now raise energy to hold in the Circle—similar to the Cone of Power we describe in appendix C's Earth Healing ritual—for later use. All join hands and dance in a circle, chanting "The Witches' Rune":

> **Darksome night and shining moon,**
> **East, then south, then west, then north,**
> **Hearken to the Witches' Rune!**
> **Here we come to call ye forth.**
>
> **Earth and Water, Air and Fire,**
> **Wand and Pentacle and Sword.**
> **Work ye unto our desire and**
> **hearken ye unto our word.**
>
> **Cords and censer, scourge and knife,**
> **Powers of the Witches' blade,**
> **Waken all ye unto life**
> **And come ye as the charm is made.**
>
> **Queen of Heaven, Queen of Hell,**
> **Hornèd Hunter of the Night,**
> **Lend your powers unto our spell**
> **And work our will by magic rite.**
>
> **By all the power of land and sea,**
> **By all the might of Moon and Sun,**
> **As we do will,**

So Mote It Be!
Chant the spell and be it done!
Eko Eko Azarak,
Eko Eko Zomelak,
Eko Eko Cernunnos!
Eko Eko Aradia!
(repeat softly once more)

This was written by Doreen Valiente and Gerald Gardner. The origin of the "Eko Eko" refrain is very cloudy and uncertain, but Stewart Farrar quotes Doreen as speculating that it came from an ancient chant, and that Azarak and Zomelak are Deity names. This is discussed in *Eight Sabbats for Witches* by Stewart and Janet Farrar.

If the God and Goddess are to be invoked, the rite is performed in the manner determined by the HPS and the HP, or other officiates. Any uninitiated participants in the Circle should now be allowed to leave the Circle after a Priest or Priestess ceremonially "cuts" a gateway in it to let them out. The Circle is then closed again.

After the Gods have been invoked, or evoked if that is the decision for this rite, allot the proper time for honoring the Gods in silence. This is a good time to offer seasonal commemorations and to perform desired or planned magic. If uninitiated participants have been cut out of the Circle for the invocations, they may be invited back in either before the magic or afterward, depending on the officiates' decision. Close the opening cut in the Circle again after they have re-entered.

Now the HPS and HP will consecrate the cakes (or cookies or bread) and wine (ale, juice), and all present will offer libations. The HP kneels at the feet of the HPS offering the chalice of wine. The HPS lowers the magical wand or Athame into the wine saying:

As above, so below;
As the Universe, so the Soul;
As within, so without.

Or a variation:

As above, so below,
As the thought, so the material manifestation.

Another frequently used variation is:

As the Athame is to the male,

So the Cup is to the female,
And conjoined they bring forth creation.

After the wine is consecrated, the HP touches the Athame to the cakes while the HPS holds the plate, saying:

O Queen most sacred,
Bless this food unto our bodies,
Bestowing health, strength, joy
And the fulfillment of love
Which is perpetual happiness.
So Mote It Be.

All may now sit in a circle to share the cakes and wine. First, each offers some wine and a piece of the cake to the Gods and Elementals, dropping it into a bowl and saying:

To the Gods, Blessed Be.

After all have had a chance to partake of the cakes and wine, the liba-tion bowl is put aside. This is a good time to teach, discuss coven needs, or simply to make merry! It is also a good time to chant and make music.

When all is finished and it is time to end the Circle, the Watchtowers are dismissed, East to East, deosil, with a banishing Pentagram and a salute at each quarter. (The banishing Pentagram of Earth is drawn essentially "backward" from the invoking, starting at the bottom left point of the star and going up.)

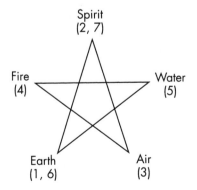

Banishing Earth Pentagram

**Bright ones of air/fire/water/earth,
Dwellers in the East/South/West/North,
We thank thee for thy protection, aid and wisdom,
And we bid thee: "Hail and farewell."**

The officiate takes up the Circle with the Athame, sword, or wand, moving around widdershins (counterclockwise), East to East. The energy is drawn up again into the body of the Priest or Priestess, and back down into the earth.

The Maiden or other appointed participant follows the officiate with a candle.

The officiating HPS, HP, or other says:

**Fire seal the Circle round,
Let it fade beneath the ground.
Magic creates reality;
As we do will,
So Mote It Be!**

All together may say:

**Merry meet and merry part and
Merry meet again!**

And thus the Circle is ended, or as Wiccan tradition teaches, open, but unbroken.

This is one form of the Wiccan Circle Casting. A great deal of training and practice goes into performing it smoothly and with the most effective visualizations. However, if you memorize it and carefully practice the various points, such as the Pentagrams, beforehand you will be able to use this form to begin creating the World Between the Worlds for your own ritual purposes.

Remember you are creating consecrated sacred space, as sacred as any cathedral or synagogue. It is a temple space of your creation for the Gods and Goddesses. Treat this space and your altar and sacred objects with care and respect. Then the work you do within it will take on deep significance in your consciousness and will ring with magical power on other planes as well. Dare I repeat it again? "As above, so below"—it works in reverse as well.

Nothing we do is insignificant if we endow it and imbue it with reverence and enlightened consciousness. Whether a sacred space is a meticulously elegant Temple of classical proportions, or a corner in a small apartment bedroom, does not matter. (Once when my family and I were in a rented house with our things in boxes in the basement, awaiting our move to a permanent home, I set up a little Temple in the corner of the bare basement, using the packing boxes as "walls." It worked very nicely.) What matters is how conscientiously you prepare the sacred space, what kind of magical intention you carry out, and most of all, how powerful your relationship with the earth, the Elementals, and the Divinity is. As the Lakota Medicine Man Lame Deer said: "The rest is just trimmings."

Appendix C

An Earth Healing Ritual

The following Circle was created with the intention of joining magically in the international commemoration of "Earth Healing Day," the unofficial but widely accepted name for April twenty-first, the day before Earth Day. I wrote this ritual in 1990 for a large event in London. Since that time I have adapted it for use in a number of different settings in the United States.

The purpose and intent of this ritual is to add our energies to the worldwide effort to aid Mother Gaia in battling the onslaught of ills besetting her, and to strengthen her healing process. We also consecrated and charged either seeds or water for each participant to take away. The participants could then plant or sprinkle the seeds or water in a place they love, or a place in need. Depending on the time of the month and the lunar tides, the focus could be healing or cleansing or banishing ills.

The original ritual was written for a large group, but it can be altered to suit any size group. I offer it to you as a final exercise and a more complex ritual, taking you further still on the path of Earth Stewardship and magical activism.

Reverencing the Earth

The altar is prepared as for any Circle, either in Wicca style or another tradition's. Also needed for the Rite is a large container of seeds or of water, enough so that each person can take some of each. You may also need containers for participants to take seeds or water away.

If there is a large crowd and it is not known how experienced the group is in working magic, then it might be wise for the High Priestess (or other designated person) to give a little introduction. She could offer some descriptions of the visualizations to be used, such as the Watchtowers, the "Cone of Power," and so on. Given that Earth Healing is the key component here, and some participants may not be experienced at magic, a very exact description of the desired magical image should be given to everyone. For example, the Cone of Power can be visualized as a shimmering blue cone of energy that, when the High Priestess signals, will fly off skyward and disappear, to merge on the astral plane with other magical energies being directed toward Earth Healing (merging with the larger group mind). If you are working this alone, you will direct the Cone of Power to go to Gaia.

When dancing beforehand to raise energy for the magic, it would be appropriate and helpful for all to visualize the earth glowing with the shimmering, etheric blue energy of healing power.

The Priest and/or Priestess prepare the sacred space and cast the Circle, call up the Watchtowers, and so on. The Priestess gives a kind of Opening "Invocation" or Evocation to state the intent and honor the Goddess and God. Whatever is desired may be invented and used. Below is a possibility (adapted from the original used in the London Circle).

> Priestess: **O Great Mother! She who is called Gaia, Rhea, Ceres, Tara, Demeter, Erce, Tellus Mater, Pachamama ... and many other names; She from whom all life springs and to whom all must return to be reborn.**
>
> **O great Horned Lord of the forests, mountains, meadows, and plains! He who is called Herne, Pan, Cernunnos, Robin, Arthur ... Comforter and consoler, hunter and hunted.**
>
> **We have seen the devastation and dishonoring of the sacred body of our mother the Earth. We have heard the cries and witnessed the pain of our fellow creatures who crawl and run, who slither, swim, and fly.**
>
> **Bless our working here, empower us, O ancient ones, that with your aid we may begin to undo the wrong and heal the pain (or "banish the pain" if it is a waning moon).**
>
> **So Mote It Be.**

(All repeat: **"So Mote It Be."**)

Now the participants will raise magical energy and send out the Cone of Power, which can be done in any way that is usual or desirable for the group. Include some dancing and chant something appropriate, perhaps a Pagan chant such as "The earth is our Mother" or "We all come from the Goddess," preferably with drumming, if drums are desired and available. Those dancing move deosil (clockwise) in a circle, dancing more and more quickly to raise the energy desired. Or if the group prefers, the High Priestess can lead everyone in a traditional Spiral Dance, which takes the form of a long line that snakes and spirals in and out, moving deosil, till the High Priestess calls the halt.

During this time, all participants should hold the image of the planet in mind. At the moment she deems "correct," the High Priestess will move into the center of the group and raise her arms. All should then cluster around her as she directs the Cone of Power up and away. All should visualize strongly to enhance the group mind's healing power.

The Priest or Priestess then consecrates the bowl of seeds, and the coven or group breaks in to four smaller circles, one at each quarter. The Priest or Priestess carries the bowl of seeds to the center of each circle. A previously chosen leader will say something to call upon the quarter for blessing and assistance. The smaller circle then uses the power of its quarter's element to charge the seeds with Earth Healing energy. If this rite is enacted by a single person, he or she will move around to each quarter, performing the blessings.

The charging can be done silently, or in any way that is desired and most effective for the group. When the seeds have been charged by the whole group, they are carried back to the main altar.

The Priest or Priestess will next bless the cakes and wine (or ale, or a nonalcoholic beverage, if preferred) in the way he or she is accustomed or chooses to work. If working with a large group, the Priest and Priestess can stand at opposite ends of the altar while the group comes up one by one, first to the Priest for a cake, then to the Priestess for a sip from the Chalice.

In a smaller group, the cakes and wine may be celebrated in whatever is the traditional way of the coven or group. (My coven traditionally sits in a circle in the middle of the sacred space, and I have done this with various groups, depending on how big the space is we are in.)

Next each person goes to the altar to take some charged seeds or some charged water from the large bowl. The participants will take and plant these seeds or sprinkle the water in a place special to them for healing of that place particularly, or for a general healing of the earth.

The Priest may say something appropriate to close and seal the intention of the group. He or another may choose to lead a chakra closing for the group, as well. Below is a closing adapted from that used in the various American Circles:

O Lady of Nature, veiled on earth, unveiled in the heavens!

Mother Gaia, bestower of prosperity, fertility and peace!

O Lord of the greenwood and of the dark—piper at the gates of dawn,

wild rider on the winds and helper of our nonhuman brethren!

O Elemental rulers and beings of East, South, West, and North!

Hear our petition, we pray! Aid us all in becoming true Rainbow Warriors, magical crusaders of spiritual activism whose weaponry is light, love, faith, beauty, and divine inspiration.

We send forth these seeds consecrated and charged with healing power to help our blessed Mother Earth in these times of need. The symbolism of the seed and of planting is that of new life and of creation. It is also a sign of faith that life will be reborn. Remembering this and commemorating this international day of Earth Healing, we seek to plant the seeds of healing and transformation.

May human consciousness be transformed to one of true Deep Ecology, of greater oneness with Nature and the All-That-Is. And may our faith make us catalysts in the healing of our precious earthly home.

So mote it be.

(And again, all repeat.)

Alternately, if water is used, the Priestess may say:

We send forth this water, consecrated and charged with healing power in aid of our blessed Mother Earth at her moment of need. Water is the element of love, its quarter the West, the place of rebirth and transformation. Remembering this, we seek for human consciousness to be transformed; thus may we aid in the transformation and healing of the ills besetting our earthly home.

So Mote It Be!

(Repeated by all.)

The Priest or Priestess bids farewell to the Watchtowers and takes up the Circle in whatever way is usual or appropriate.

This has been a very adaptable ceremony in format, and people love to have the specially consecrated and magically endowed seeds or water.

In a similar style, one year in Denver for Earth Day the United Religions Initiative and other multidenominational groups organized a large, public, multifaith ceremony. Consecrated seeds were given out in little packets. It is lovely symbolism, as well as a good service for the earth—both physically, in planting new flowers, herbs, and other plants, and metaphysically. At this unique and memorable ceremony in Denver's Currigan Hall, with many denominations present, my coven and I were asked to lead the group in charging four young trees with healing energy, which were then planted in the four corners of Colorado. It was a moving and beautiful ceremony, not only for its Earth Healing commitment, but also for the heartwarming ecumenical collaboration of extremely diverse faiths working together.

Recommended Reading

Abbey, Edward. *Desert Solitaire*. New York and Toronto: Ballantine, 1977 (1968, 1971).

———. *The Monkey Wrench Gang*. New York: HarperCollins Perennial, 2000 (1975, 1985).

Bates, Brian. *The Way of the Actor—A Path to Knowledge and Power*. Boston: Shambhala, 1988.

Beston, Henry. *The Outermost House*. New York: Henry Holt & Co., 1988.

Bonewits, Ra. *The Cosmic Crystal Spiral*. London: Element Books, 1987.

Boone, J. Allen. *Kinship with All Life*. New York: Harper & Row, 1954.

Bradley, Marion Zimmer. *The Lady of Avalon*. New York: Penguin, 1997.

———. *The Mists of Avalon*. New York: Knopf, 1983.

Brennan, Barbara Ann. *Hands of Light—A Guide to Healing through the Human Energy Field*. New York: Bantam Books, 1987.

Carr-Gomm, Philip. *The Druid Renaissance—The Voice of Druidry Today*. Ed. Philip Carr-Gomm. London: Thorsons, 1996.

———. *The Druid Tradition*. Shaftesbury, Dorset: Element Books, 1991.

Crowley, Vivianne. *Principles of Wicca*. London: Thorsons, 1997.

———. *Wicca—The Old Religion in the New Age*. Northamptonshire: Thorsons, 1989; rev. as *Wicca—The Old Religion in the New Millennium*. London: Thorsons, 1996.

———. *A Woman's Kabbalah—Kabbalah for the 21st Century*. London: Thorsons, 2000.

Devall, Bill, and George Sessions. *Deep Ecology—Living as If Nature Mattered*. Layton, UT: Gibbs Smith, 1985

Dobson, Andrew, ed. *The Green Reader*. London: Andre Deutsch Ltd., 1991.

Estes, Clarissa Pinkola. *Women Who Run with the Wolves—Myths and Stories of the Wild Woman Archetype*. New York: Ballantine Books, 1992.

Farrar, Janet, and Stewart Farrar. *Eight Sabbats for Witches*. London: Robert Hale, 1981.

———. *Spells and How They Work*. London: Robert Hale, 1990.

Fields, Rick, Rex Weyler, Rick Ingrasci, and Peggy Taylor. *Chop Wood, Carry Water*. Los Angeles: Tarcher, 1984.

Fortune, Dion. *Moon Magic*. York Beach, ME: Weiser, 1994 (1956).

———. *The Mystical Qabalah.* London: Aquarian Press, 1987.

———. *The Sea Priestess.* Northamptonshire: Thorsons, 1989.

Gardner, Gerald. *Witchcraft Today.* New York: Magical Childe, 1991.

Gray, William G. Inner *Traditions of Magic.* York Beach, ME: Weiser, 1984 (1970, 1978).

Harner, Michael. *The Way of the Shaman.* New York: Harper & Row, 1990 (1980).

Hoffman, Chris. *The Hoop and the Tree—A Compass for Finding a Deeper Relationship with all Life.* San Francisco, CA, and Tulsa, OK: Council Oak Books, 2000.

Holbeche, Soozi. *The Power of Gems and Crystals.* London: Piatkus Books, 1995.

Jung, C. G. *Memories, Dreams, Reflections.* New York: Vintage Books, 1989 (orig. pub. Random House, 1963).

Lovelock, J. E. *Gaia: A New Look at Life on Earth.* Oxford: Oxford University Press, 1987 (1979).

Macy, Joanna. *Coming Back to Life—Practices to Reconnect Our Lives, Our World.* British Columbia & Stony Creek, CT: New Society Publishers, 1998.

Macy, Joanna, Pat Fleming, Arne Naess, and John Seed. *Thinking Like a Mountain.* London: Heretic Books and New Society Publishers, 1988.

Manning, Al. *Helping Yourself with White Witchcraft.* West Nyack, NY: Parker, 1974 (1972).

Matthews, William. *Geology Made Simple.* New York: Doubleday & Co., 1990.

Morwyn. *Green Magic.* West Chester, PA: Whitford Press, 1994.

———. *Web of Light: Rites for Witches in the New Age.* Atglen, PA: Whitford Press, 1993.

Nelkon, M. *Principles of Atomic Physics and Electronics,* 5th ed. London: Heinemann Educational, 1982.

Parfitt, Will. *The Qabalah.* Shaftesbury, Dorset: Element Books, 1991.

Perera, Sylvia Brinton. *Descent to the Goddess—A Way of Initiation for Women.* Toronto: Inner City Books, 1981.

Rael, Joseph E. *Beautiful Painted Arrow.* Shaftesbury, Dorset: Element Books, 1992.

Raphael, Katrina. *Crystal Enlightenment,* vols. 1 & 2. New York: Aurora Press, 1985.

Ravenwolf, Silver. *To Ride a Silver Broomstick—New Generation Witchcraft*. St. Paul, MN: Llewellyn, 1994.

Reed, Ellen Cannon. *The Goddess and the Tree*. St. Paul, MN: Llewellyn, 1993.

Roszak, Theodore. *The Voice of the Earth*. New York: Simon & Schuster, 1992.

Roszak, Theodore, Mary E. Gomes, and Allen D. Kanner. *Ecopsychology—Restoring the Earth, Healing the Mind*. New York: Sierra Club Books, Crown Publishers, 1995.

Russell, Peter. *The Awakening Earth*. London: Arkana, Routledge, 1982.

Schneider, Michael S. *A Beginner's Guide to Constructing the Universe*. New York: HarperCollins, 1995 (1994).

Schoen, Allen M., and Pam Proctor. *Love, Miracles and Animal Healing*. New York:, Simon & Schuster, Fireside, 1995.

Sessions, George, ed. *Deep Ecology for the 21st Century*. Boston, MA: Shambhala, 1995.

Silbey, Uma. *The Complete Crystal Guidebook*. San Francisco, CA: U-Read Publications, 1986.

Slater, Herman. *A Book of Pagan Rituals*. York Beach, ME: Weiser, 1978.

Starhawk. *Dreaming the Dark*. Boston, MA: Beacon Press, 1982

———. *The Spiral Dance: A Rebirth of the Ancient Religion of the Great Goddess*. San Francisco, CA: Harper & Row, 1979.

Stepanich, Kisma K. *The Gaia Tradition*. St. Paul, MN: Llewellyn, 1991.

Thoreau, Henry. *The Portable Thoreau*. New York: Viking Press, 1964 (1947, 1962).

Valiente, Doreen. *Witchcraft for Tomorrow*. London: Robert Hale, 1978.

Walker, Barbara. *The Women's Encyclopedia of Myths and Secrets*. San Francisco, CA: Harper & Row, 1983.

———. *Women's Rituals—A Sourcebook*. San Francisco, CA: Harper & Row, 1990.

Whitcomb, Bill. *The Magician's Companion*. St. Paul, MN: Llewellyn, 1994.

Endnotes

1. This recent movement stresses a reborn deep and holy connection with Nature, a true Christian Deep Ecology. It draws from such sources as the early Hebrew and Christian texts and medieval mystics, as well as indigenous cultures around the world. Creation Spirituality was made famous in the 1970s and 1980s by theologian Matthew Fox, who founded the University of Creation Spirituality in California. Today Dr. Fox is an Episcopal priest and the author of many inspiring books on this Earth-honoring, mystical tradition of Christianity.

2. Two decades later they are still at it. For example, Starhawk and other Witches were arrested in the huge protests at Seattle's WTO convention in November 1999. Starhawk does not call herself Wiccan, although she is an Initiate, but is proudly a Witch and an Ecofeminist activist. We all owe her a debt of gratitude and admiration for her courage.

3. Vivianne Crowley, "The Pipes of Pan," in *Wicca: The Old Religion in the New Millennium* (London: Thorsons, 1996), p. 154.

4. For a most marvelous work and guidebook for learning to sense and work with this energy field, see *Hands of Light* by Barbara Ann Brennan. Dr. Brennan has created a school of study on healing through working with what she calls the Human Energy Field, or HEF.

5. The psychological and magical concept of "group mind" is explored further in chapter 7 in connection with Earth Healing magic. In brief, the expression refers to the linked consciousness that can develop among people who work together intensely, the interconnection of the minds on various levels. This can sometimes be witnessed in people who spend a lot of time together, in office situations, in schools, on sports teams, in families.

6. From the workshop "Rocking with Your Cosmic Rocks," created by Francesca Ciancimino Howell, aka Gwendyth Erce, and given in the U.K., Germany, and the United States, 1990–1995.